Y0-BRL-485

THE ANALYSIS OF POLITICAL CLEAVAGES

THE ANALYSIS OF
POLITICAL CLEAVAGES

by Douglas W. Rae and Michael Taylor

NEW HAVEN AND LONDON, YALE UNIVERSITY PRESS, 1970

CONTENTS

PREFACE

This small book is offered in the knowledge that its readership will be small and in the hope that its useful lifetime will be brief. It is written for our colleagues in political science and political sociology who are already committed to the development of a political theory which is genuinely comparative and firmly grounded in empirical realities. The aim is methodological: to offer more precise and more general interpretations than now exist for some central concepts in the study of cleavage systems. These concepts — fragmentation, intensity, cross-cutting — organize the essay. We are inclined to believe that our analyses of fragmentation and cross-cutting will be more likely to stand up than our treatment of intensity, which is a frankly preliminary attack on a virtually intractable problem.

We are grateful to Joseph LaPalombara and William Riker for their help. Financial aid for parts of the project has come from Yale University, the University of Essex, and the John Simon Guggenheim Foundation. Permissions have been granted by "Comparative Politics" and "Polity" for material appearing here as parts of the third and fourth chapters.

The last word is for Hugh Rae, who, even at age two, saw fit to destroy various parts of earlier drafts, and for Aubrey Garlington, who condemned the project on aesthetic grounds. They were right of course. Millions of other people stood by indifferently.

D.W.R.
M.T.

East Bergholt and Wivenhoe
November 1969

vii

CHAPTER 1: CLEAVAGES

The latent causes of faction are ... sown in the nature of man; and we see them everywhere brought into different degrees of activity, according to the different circumstances of civil society. A zeal for different opinions concerning religion, concerning government ... an attachment to different leaders ambitiously contending for pre-eminence and power; or to persons of other descriptions whose fortunes have been interesting to the human passions, have, in turn, divided mankind into parties, inflamed them with mutual animosity, and rendered them much more disposed to vex and oppress each other than to cooperate for the common good.[1]

Cleavages are the criteria which divide the members of a community or subcommunity into groups, and the relevant cleavages are those which divide members into groups with important political differences at specific times and places. These cleavages fall into three general classes: (1) ascriptive or "trait" cleavages such as race or caste; (2) attitudinal or "opinion" cleavages such as ideology or, less grandly, preference; and (3) behavioral or "act" cleavages such as those elicited through voting and organizational membership. Each individual may find himself set apart from others by ascriptive, attitudinal, and behavioral cleavages—his race, his attitude toward racial segregation, and his S.C.L.C. membership, for example.

These three classes of cleavages are commonly dignified by separate terms. Cleavage by traits determines the "heterogeneity" or "homogeneity" of a community. Cleavage by attitude determines the extent of "dissensus"

1. James Madison, The Federalist, number 10.

1

or "consensus" in a community. And cleavage by behavior determines the "fractionalization" or "cohesion"
of a community. Each of these dichotomies is generally
thought to specify the poles of a continuum. One thinks,
therefore, of the extent to which people exhibit similar
traits, attitudes, or behaviors as corresponding to the extent of homogeneity, consensus, and cohesion in that community. The three resulting continua are these:

Type of Criterion	Low Cleavage Extreme	High Cleavage Extreme
Traits	Homogeneity	Heterogeneity
Attitudes	Consensus	Dissensus
Behaviors	Cohesion	Fractionalization

The definitional boundaries between these three continua can be no clearer than the distinctions between traits,
attitudes, and behaviors. Consider religious cleavages,
for example. Is one's religion an ascriptive trait, a complex of attitudes, or the artifact of a behavior such as join-
ing a congregation? To answer this question, we would
need to cope not only with the theologians, but also with
the sociologists of religion. In this and many other cases,
it is necessary to stipulate arbitrarily that a given cleavage belongs to the domain of trait, attitude, or behavior
and therefore aligns itself with the heterogeneity–homogeneity, dissensus-consensus, or cohesion–fractionalization continuum. Fortunately, the arbitrariness of these
classifications is often not very important; it certainly is
not important to our metrical analysis.

This is because each is a continuum subsumed in the
more general problem of cleavage, and each gives rise to
an identical set of formal questions:

1. Into how many subgroups does this cleavage divide
   this population?
2. How are these people distributed among the subgroups?

3. With what degree of intensity does each person cleave to his subgroup?[2]
4. How are individual positions on one cleavage related to positions on another cleavage?

These formal questions give rise to five theoretically interesting properties of cleavages and cleavage systems. Each of these five properties, as the reader will recognize, plays a part in explanatory political theory.

1. Crystallization: What proportion of a community finds itself committed to any recognizable position on a given cleavage? Crystallization sets the outer boundary of cleavage.

Within the crystallized portion of the community, two additional properties arise.

2. Fragmentation: To what degree does this cleavage set the members of the community against each other? Or, more exactly, how many pairs of members find themselves at odds over any given cleavage?
3. The intensity of fragmentation: With what intensity does this cleavage set the members of a community against each other? Or, more exactly, what proportion of the pairs which are divided at all by a cleavage will be divided with a given degree of intensity?

If we consider relationships between cleavages, two further properties claim attention.

2. The exact nature of intensity depends on the type of cleavage. For trait cleavages, intensity corresponds to the political importance attached by each individual to his possession of that trait. For attitudes, intensity means just what the social psychologists suggest — the strength with which an individual holds his opinion. For behaviors, intensity refers to the political significance the individual attaches to his action. See section 1.2 below for an elaboration of this and related points.

4. The degree of overlap: To what extent is the crystallized portion of the community on one cleavage the same as the crystallized portion on another?
5. The degree of cross-cutting: To what extent do two cleavages divide a community along different axes? Or, more exactly, to what extent may we expect pairs divided by one cleavage to be united by another, and vice versa?

If it is admitted for the moment that these are theoretically important properties of cleavages and cleavage systems, it must also be confessed that they are vague and imprecise.   Each of these properties figures in almost every part of political science, and each is potentially subject to exact theoretical usage. Yet there presently exists no conceptual system which gives quantitative precision to these concepts. The purpose of this book is to provide a conceptual analysis which yields simple, theoretically interpreted values for each of the five properties of cleavages and cleavage systems (how much crystallization, what degree of fragmentation, what intensity of fragmentation, how much overlap, and what degree of cross-cutting).   Before we proceed with the analysis itself, it may be useful to illustrate the theoretical importance of our enterprise.

1.1 On the Theoretical Importance of Measuring the Extent and Intensity of Political Division

It is, as we have said, obvious that the divisions created by political cleavages are important to politics and political theory.   Much of contemporary democratic theory is based on certain rather special presumptions about cleavage and division (see below). The "group theory of politics," as its enemies call it, is little more than an argument that certain special forms of organized fragmentation are powerful forces in the politics of a few advanced industrial nations (Bentley 1908; Truman 1951). Were there not a certain dissensus on actual and imagined public policies or allocations, Harold Lasswell's famous

5

question— "Who gets what, when, how?"— would appear trivial (Lasswell 1936). In a perverse way "structural-functionalism" begins with some very restrictive assumptions about the extent and desirability of division (Levy 1952; Almond 1960). And games, as defined in game theory, are predicated upon the presence of various types of cleavage— or conflicts of interest— between players (Luce and Raiffa 1957, for example). Cleavages are, in short, important to almost every branch of political theory.

It is somewhat less obvious that we must treat cleavages with high precision. Obviously no treatment of cleavages and cleavage systems, however exact it may be, will amount to a general theory of politics. And it may be supposed that intuitive analyses of cleavages will suffice for many purposes. Any sweeping argument to the contrary— to the effect that exact analysis is always necessary— is not apt to be very helpful. It may be more useful to examine a few theoretical problems for the specific applications an exact analysis of cleavages may have in their solution. These examples may help to establish the point that some important theoretical positions can be advanced only by an exact analysis of cleavages.

For this purpose we have singled out three specific problems, each of which happens to belong to the loosely knit family of ideas which calls itself "democratic theory." The first of these is James Madison's well-known but unverified hypothesis relating the size and diversity of political communities to the occurrence of cohesive and tyrannical majorities. The second is the well-known problem which arises in the confrontation of intense minorities and apathetic majorities. And the third is a variant of the pluralist argument on the preconditions of democratic political organization. In each of these instances we will show that only with an exact means of analyzing political cleavages can we surpass common sense in approaching the problem.

Madison's hypothesis

Toward the end of Federalist 10, after Madison has completed his argument for republicanism, he turns to the relative merits of large and small republics. He is, of course, arguing polemically for a large republic—that is, the United States as established by the Constitution of 1787. He begins with the trivial argument that big countries have more people, are therefore apt to have more good people, and can accordingly expect to find more good leaders. But Madison himself seems aware that this argument is a weak one, and he turns abruptly to another:

> The smaller the country, the fewer probably will be the distinct parties and interests composing it; the fewer the distinct parties and interests, the more frequently will a majority be found of the same party; and the smaller the number of individuals composing a majority, and the smaller the compass within which they are placed, the more easily will they concert and execute their plans of oppression. Extend the sphere and you take in a greater variety of parties and interests; you make it less probable that a majority of the whole will have a common motive to invade the rights of other citizens; it will be more difficult for all who feel it to discover their own strength, and to act in unison with each other.

A close examination of this passage and the larger argument in which it is embedded suggests that there are at least seven operative, extralogical terms, connected by causal inferences in support of a polemical assertion. The seven operative terms are:

1. The geographic extent of the electorate
2. The number of people in the electorate
3. The diversity of interests in the electorate
4. The diversity of organized factions in the electorate
5. The existence (or nonexistence) of a majority faction
6. The cohesion of the majority faction if it exists
7. The imposition (or nonimposition) of tyrannical

policies (presumably by cohesive majority factions)[3]

These seven terms are combined at two levels—in a proposition, and in an explanatory model meant to connect its two operative terms. Briefly, the argument is this:

> Proposition: Large republics are less subject to tyrannical policies than small republics.
> Definition: Large republics are those which possess numerous and extended electorates.

This is so because either

> A. The more extended the electorate, the greater the diversity of interests within it [1→ 3]

or

> B. The more numerous the electorate, the greater the diversity of interests within it [2 → 3]

or both. And

> C. The more diverse the interests within the electorate, the more diverse the organized factions within it [3 → 4].

3. Robert A. Dahl restates the same passage as follows: "To the extent that the electorate is numerous, extended, and diverse in interests, a majority faction is less likely to exist, and if it does exist, is less likely to act as a unity" (Dahl 1956, pp. 17, 33). This statement combines the third and fourth terms of our interpretation (diversity of interests and of organized factions) under the term "diverse in interests," and it lets the seventh term (tyrannical policy) be assumed from the context of his and Madison's arguments. Which of these two interpretations is closer to Madison's intent we cannot say. More important for our purposes is the fact that the seven-term interpretation gives a fuller argument, more readily amenable to verification.

And

    D. The more diverse the organized factions in the electorate, the less likely is a majority faction to exist [4→5]

or

    E. The more diverse the organized factions in the electorate, the less cohesive the majority faction, if it exists [4→6]

or both. And

    F. If there is no majority faction, tyrannical policies are less likely to be adopted [5→7]

or

    G. The less cohesive the majority faction, if it exists, the less likely it is to impose tyrannical policies [6→7].

The proposition connects variables 1 and 2 (extent and numerousness of the electorate) with variable 7 (tyrannical policy) by means of the model described in these seven hypotheses (A–G). This model is pictured in fig. 1.1.

Figure 1.1

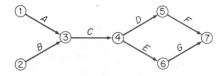

Now this model is very flexible indeed. It contains six variants, or paths, which are each sufficient to sustain the main proposition: ACDF, BCDF, ABCDF, ACEG, BCEG, and ABCEG. If any one of these obtains, then we can expect large republics to be relatively tyranny-proof. And even by the best standards of contemporary social science, Madison's argument here, as elsewhere, is well worth careful investigation.

The catch is this: all the model's variants contain at least three hypotheses which cannot be tested without the aid of a general and precise measure for the extent of division over certain cleavages. This is because the two centrally located variables (3 and 4) are based on cleavage concepts of the kind analyzed in this book. Variable 3 requires some measure for the diversity of interests in the electorate, and variable 4 requires some measure for the diversity of organized factions. We must know, in other words, how extensively these two as yet undefined forms of cleavage divide the electorate. In addition, three of the model's variants (ACEG, BCEG, and ABCEG) contain four hypotheses requiring a measure for the extent of division, because they pass through variable 6, the cohesion of majority factions.

Perhaps the need for a general and precise means of measuring the extent of division explains the fact that this very well-known argument remains the property of folklore, not social science. In chapter 2 we develop a measure which we think will allow us to do useful analyses of arguments containing diversity terms. And we apply this measure to Madison's model.

Dahl on the intensity of divisions

In his **Preface to Democratic Theory**, Robert A. Dahl has written a very lucid but necessarily inconclusive account of "the problem of intensity" (Dahl 1956, pp. 90–123). Suppose we have a political community which is divided by a series of policy questions. Each of these questions divides the community into at least two nominal groups: those for a proposal and those against it.[4] Each

4. It is possible to find more than two nominal groups when, for example, each question generates several proposals. Later we will consider some of these more complex cases, but here let us confine ourselves to Dahl's two-group cases. See also Rae and Taylor 1969.

individual cleaves to his nominal position with a given degree of intensity. For the resulting divisions, Dahl adduces frequency distributions in the form shown in fig. 1.2.

Figure 1.2

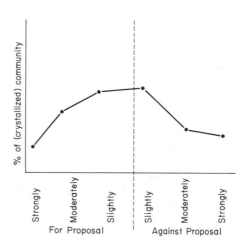

Dahl examines a series of these frequency curves, asking two kinds of questions about them. First he considers what effect certain divisions are apt to have on the stability of "polyarchal"[5] political organizations. If, as

5. By polyarchy, Dahl means something like "representative democracy," defined by eight norms: (1) all members vote, (2) their votes count about equally, (3) the most popular alternative wins, (4) members may insert alternatives, (5) all members have the same information about alternatives, (6) alternatives with the greatest number of votes displace any alternatives with fewer votes, (7) orders of elected officials are effectuated, and (8) the policies carried out are subordinate to or executory of the voting decisions mentioned above. Alternatives are leaders or policies. For a much more exact definition, see Dahl 1956, pp. 63–85, or Dahl and Lindblom 1953, pp. 277–79. For most purposes, we may say that polyarchy and democratic political organization are the same thing.

Dahl plausibly suggests, some divisions are apt to result in civil strife and others are not, the interesting problem becomes, "How do we go about establishing the threshold at which polyarchal regimes can no longer be expected to resolve policy divisions peaceably?"[6] But the exact comparisons implied by this question are not possible without a metrical system for analyzing the intensities of divisions. This we may call the "stability problem."[7]

Second, Dahl considers the especially vexing case of "severe asymmetrical disagreement," in which an intense minority is set apart by some policy cleavage from an apathetic majority.

Figure 1.3

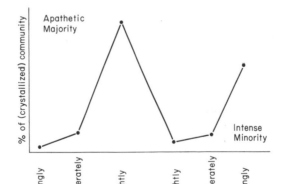

6. Dahl holds that divisions of the kind pictured in our illustrative curve are apt to result in civil strife. This is plausible, but it does not tell us how much the division must resemble the one pictured if it is to produce trouble. Dahl 1956, pp. 97–99.

7. For Dahl's more recent thinking on the problem of stability, see "Who Governs?" (1961). See also Budge 1970.

Under simple majority rule, we are compelled to say that the minority gives way to the majority, no matter how intense the former or how apathetic the latter. Dahl asks, "Would it be possible to construct rules so that an apathetic majority only slightly preferring its alternative could not override a minority strongly preferring its alternative?" (Dahl 1956, p. 92). This question is deceptively straightforward, since it does not tell us how large and apathetic the majority or how small and intense the minority. But without a conceptual and metrical scheme of the kind we present for the intensity of divisions, it is not possible to pose the question more exactly. We will later call this the "minorities problem."

The paucity of useful data and the difficulty of measuring intensity even on the basis of externals prevent an empirical extension of Dahl's analysis. But, even if these data were readily available, existing techniques of analysis would prohibit a rigorous theoretical interpretation of the findings. In chapter 3, we present a metrical system for analyzing the intensities of divisions and apply it to Dahl's hypothetical cases.

The cross-cutting cleavages hypothesis

Democratic political organization is a fragile arrangement which seems to work only in certain kinds of social settings. By "democratic political organization," we usually mean something like "political regimes which resolve the problem of succession by means of regular, open, and usually partisan elections, and which therefore legitimate the right of opposition." We see that representative democracies of this kind have worked stably in the English-speaking countries, Scandinavia, and a major portion of lower western Europe. And we also observe that this kind of organization has not worked stably in most other nations. In some of these—the USSR, for example—representative democracy was never really begun. In others, such as Spain, it was begun but collapsed. In still others—France, for instance—representative democracy has appeared, disappeared, and reappeared.

These differences create an urgent and interesting theoretical problem for political scientists and political sociologists: What are the preconditions for democratic political organization? Answers to this question are both numerous and various. Some observers, from Montesquieu to Huntington, have gone so far as to suggest that temperate climates stimulate democratic organization—a correlationally correct but theoretically barren assertion. By far the largest number of theories locate the conditions of democratic organization in the admittedly vast domain of social structure. From Marx to Lipset, these theorists have called attention to a society's system of cleavages or one of its aspects. What results is not a theory, but a mixed catalogue of hypotheses about connections between cleavage systems and political organization. Each of these hypotheses would be more helpful if it were more exactly formulated.

This may be illustrated by examining the often-repeated hypothesis that cross-cutting cleavages conduce to lasting democratic political organization, whereas reinforcing systems of cleavage tend to undermine it.[8] Amazingly enough, we have no precise theoretical definition of cross-cutting cleavages. Roughly, cross-cutting cleavages assure that those persons who are divided by one cleavage (say, race) will be brought together by another (say, religion) and vice versa.[9] Reinforcing cleavages, by way of contrast, assure that those who are divided by one cleavage (race) will also be divided by another (religion). In our example, reinforcement might result in a confrontation between white Protestants and black Catholics, leaving no white Catholics or black Protestants. The argument runs to the effect that this pattern

8. Leading contemporary statements of the cross-cutting cleavages argument include Truman 1951; Coser 1956; Kornhauser 1959; and Lijphart 1968. The main arguments are briefly reviewed in chapter 4 below.

9. In chapter 4 we will show that the extreme case of cross-cutting in which all pairs of people united by one cleavage are divided by the other and vice versa is a logical impossibility.

produces conflicts so intractable that they undermine the legitimacy of opposition, and that this in turn leads to the destruction of democratic political organization.

This contention would be simple enough if cleavages either did or did not cross-cut each other. Unfortunately, it is evident that virtually all extant cleavage systems result in some cross-cutting and that none result in complete cross-cutting: the pertinent question is not whether cleavages cross-cut each other, but rather how much they cross-cut each other. Further, the cross-cutting hypothesis is quite trivial unless it is related to the extent of fragmentation produced by the component cleavages. This, of course, suggests that the cross-cutting hypothesis cannot be seriously advanced unless it is embedded in an analysis which permits precise comparisons of degree for both the extent of fragmentation and the extent of cross-cutting. In chapter 4, we suggest a means of making exactly such comparisons.

Summary

We have examined the outer surfaces of three theoretical knots: Madison's diversity hypothesis, Dahl's analysis of intensity curves for policy cleavages, and the cross-cutting cleavages hypothesis. Each of these seems interesting enough to merit extensive and rigorous analysis, yet in each instance a fairly precise analysis of political cleavages appears necessary. We hope that the problems raised by these theoretically important cases will induce the reader to follow the analysis outlined in the remainder of this book.

1.2 A Basic Assumption of This Analysis

We have been assuming that cleavages sort the members of a community into mutually exclusive, nominal groups. Thus we suppose that an individual belongs to only one group on a given cleavage, and that this group is defined by its qualitative difference from all other groups. While both of these suppositions are plausible enough, it is important to recognize that neither is incontrovertible.

Not all divisions produce mutually exclusive groupings. Linguistic cleavages, for example, seldom produce mutually exclusive groups, for many individuals may be multilingual and belong therefore to several groups at once. Or consider opinion cleavages, where an individual may commit himself to a class of two or more alternatives instead of to some single alternative. And organizational cleavages — party systems, for example— may make it possible for an individual to join more than one group. [10] We must be careful, therefore, not to suppose that all cleavages produce mutually exclusive groups.

Nevertheless, the assumption of mutual exclusivity seems serviceable for most purposes. Many cleavages do produce mutually exclusive groups. This is the case with most traits such as race or religion. Moreover, most opinion cleavages lead individuals to side with some single alternative or not to take sides at all. And most party systems (though not all associational divisions) tend to approximate the condition of mutual exclusivity, at any single point in time.

Furthermore, many deviations from mutual exclusivity are rather superficial politically. A French Canadian may speak English in addition to French, but this does not mean that he is likely to behave as anything other than a member of the political group defined by his mother tongue. Most opinion cleavages lead the majority of people to some first choice, and these choices in effect produce mutually exclusive groups. And, in most political conflicts between membership organizations, each individual is apt to have one loyalty which outweighs whatever competing commitments he may have. We may conclude, then, that the assumption of mutually exclusive groups is a serviceable, if imperfect, descriptive position.

10. This is possible, for example, with electoral systems which provide for cumulative voting, or with financial contributions to two or more parties, depending upon one's conception of party membership.

Equally basic to our analysis is the assumption that cleavages distribute individuals over nominal groups rather than arraying them over ordinal or cardinal scales. In general, this assumption corresponds to the way people define their own positions. In the West, at any rate, it is common for us to say that we "belong to" a given race or organization, or that we "are for" some given public policy proposal — our identifications tend to be nominal.[11]

A first apparent exception is the alleged continuum which arrays people between left- and right-wing political ideologies. While this ordination is real enough for many participants and observers of politics, and mainly European politics, it certainly suggests more information than is actually present in most political disputes. We feel safer in presuming only that ideologies are nominal alternatives leading to nominal cleavages which may or may not be orderable from Left to Right.[12]

A second example arises from wealth and income, which produce perfect cardinal arrays of individuals and families in all money economies. While money does generate a more than nominal array, its specifically political implications are generally confined to the nominal distinctions between classes, which are defined over wealth, income, and other criteria. What counts politically is not that an individual's annual income is exactly $6,341.42, but that he defines himself as a member of the working (or middle) class. For our purposes, at least, the nominal treatment of economic status seems more sensible than would a full array by exact wealth or income.

A third example arises in investigations of voting in legislatures and other assemblies. Here it is often as-

11. In Professor Dahl's analysis (see figs. 2 and 3) the basic nominal division lies between those who favor and those who oppose a proposal. In our analysis, ordinations of intensities occur within these nominal groups.

12. See Converse (chapter 9 in Jennings and Zeigler 1966). Using Coombs's unfolding technique on some data on party preferences, Converse shows that voters in France and Finland do not all perceive their parties as ordered in a single dimension.

sumed that an abstention is a position between and on the same single dimension as affirmative and negative votes and, furthermore, that it is exactly midway between them (since votes are usually scored -1, 0, $+1$, or some other scores at equal intervals). In many cases, however, an abstention is not an expression of indifference on the issue; nor does it mean that the voter is torn equally between voting for and against. Rather, he might feel that the proposal is in some sense irrelevant; he might see the issue in such a different light that, although he has strong feelings on it, he does not relate himself to the proposal in question and cannot vote for or against it. All that is important, politically, is that there are three nominal groups. Measures of agreement, for example, based on stronger assumptions are likely to be misleading.[13]

Our assumption of mutually exclusive nominal groups is not only serviceable, as we have already argued, but also, we hope, instructive. Cleavages which divide men into groups with different preferences generate the conflicts which constitute the political process. Some of these divisions may possess more than nominal properties, but all of them are subject to instructive analysis at the nominal level, and most of those which are relevant to politics may be understood only at the nominal level.[14]

This is not to say that our analysis gives no attention to the ordering of intensities within nominal groups. These orderings are discussed in chapter 3.

1.3 The Logical Standing of This Analysis

In his Fundamentals of Concept Formation in Empirical Science (1952), Carl G. Hempel classifies the concepts by certain of their logical properties. Since Hempel's distinctions are both useful and well known, we can profitably apply a few of them to our work. First,

13. See Brams and O'Leary 1968 for a discussion of some of these measures.

14. Appendix B presents some analyses which presume more than nominal orderings.

Hempel distinguishes between real and nominal[15] definitions: real definitions purport to specify the essential properties of a thing itself, but nominal definitions rely on the interposition of other concepts. Hempel suggests that "a nominal definition may be characterized as a stipulation to the effect that a specified expression, the definiendum, is to be synonymous with a certain other expression, the definiens, whose meaning is already determined" (Hempel 1952, p. 2). Our concepts for the properties of cleavages and cleavage systems will take this nominal form, and our notation will provide the language for the "definiens" — the known concepts used to define the "definiendum." The major chapters of the book — 2, 3, and 4 — are thus to be seen as efforts to establish unambiguous connections between known concepts ("definiens") and proposed concepts ("definiendum").

Hempel also distinguishes three broad classes of concepts: (1) classificatory, (2) comparative, and (3) quantitative or metrical (Hempel 1952, pp. 50–62). These classes of concepts are listed in order of increasing precision and flexibility. Our analysis is an attempt to substitute quantitative concepts for classificatory ones. Aside from increasing the formal precision of analysis, this substitution should offer three distinct advantages. First, the quantitative concepts will allow us to discriminate between cases which classificatory concepts lump together. Second, quantitative concepts may be more useful than classificatory ones in formulating general relationships. And third, quantitative concepts may facilitate the application of mathematics to our subject. If any of these general advantages apply to the present substitution, we think that the effort will have been worthwhile.

Following Hempel once more, we may distinguish between fundamental and derived measurement. Ours is clearly a case of derived measurement under Hempel's definition: "By derived measurement we understand the

15. Note that the term "nominal" is used here in a very different sense from that in section 1.2.

determination of a metrical scale by means of criteria which presuppose at least one previous scale of measurement" (Hempel 1952, pp. 69–70). Our measures are derived since they presume that (1) members of communities can be classified by traits, attitudes, or behaviors, and (2) in some cases it is possible to assign intensity ranks within the divisions so created. While we will comment ad hoc on the problems of measurement raised by specific instances,[16] our analysis does not itself focus on the problems of fundamental measurement.

Having said this much, it is pretty clear that we cannot pretend that the resulting concepts will be synonymous with common uses of the words we use to label them. We certainly could not hope to build the logical properties just mentioned into these concepts if we were bound by the lexical definitions of these words. This means that we must content ourselves with stipulative definitions, which indicate the uses we intend to give a word without paying any particular respect to the uses others have already given them. Hence, our use of the word "fragmentation" or the word "cleavage" will not correspond to the uses given them in "The New York Times," much less in "Playboy."

We have, then, committed ourselves to four decisions. First, we will content ourselves with nominal definitions, which make no claim to direct referents in empirical reality but refer instead to other symbols. Second, we propose to generate quantitative (or metrical) concepts, as opposed to classificatory or comparative ones. Third, we will rely for our empirical referents on measures other than those which we propose: for this reason our concepts are examples of derived, not fundamental, measurement. Last, we must be content to offer stipulative

16. Examples of these difficulties are: (1) the problem of measuring the intervals between intensity ranks, and (2) the problem of multiple-trait cases in nominal classification, such as the one raised by multilinguals in the analysis of linguistic cleavages.

definitions having no determinate relationship to the ordinary uses of words.

Quite apart from the previous considerations, we must ask the more fundamental question of whether the concepts which we have chosen to analyze will prove to be useful and necessary to the development of theory. For the final test of the value of any set of concepts lies in the success of the theories in which they are employed.

The explication of concepts is certainly instructive in itself. A great deal of effort has been expended on the notion of power, for example; and now that a variety of concepts of power have been distinguished, and "power" itself has been distinguished from "influence" and "authority," the word is used more carefully. Despite the new understanding of power, however, the concept has not been used in any theory (on a reasonably strict view of "theory"). We are able to formulate hypotheses more precisely, and consequently we are able to test them. This alone would seem to justify the efforts to provide precise definitions, since a theory will be built upon those hypotheses which are accepted. But we have no guarantee that these hypotheses will be useful in developing a theory; they might be answers to wrong questions—questions which were partly prompted by the concepts they use. "Every conceptualization," says Kaplan, "involves an inductive risk. The concepts in terms of which we pose our scientific questions limit the range of admissible answers" (Kaplan 1964, p. 53). And so it is that "the proper concepts are needed to formulate a good theory, but we need a good theory to arrive at the proper concepts" (Kaplan 1964, p. 53).

The concepts which are developed in the following chapters are already prominent, in loose forms, in a number of well-known hypotheses, and some collections of these hypotheses are known as theories. Examples of these were given in the last section. Whether they really are theories, in a strict sense, is a question which can be answered only after their constituent statements (and concepts) are made precise.

The present venture is therefore a risky one. But it is difficult to believe that no partial theory of politics will find these cleavage concepts useful, at least initially, since politics arises from the existence of cleavages. And if our definitions make possible the development of a theory, which subsequently leads to the definite rejection of the concepts as inadequate, then very real progress will have been made.

CHAPTER 2: DIVERSITY

The simplest and most central attribute of a political cleavage is the extent to which it fragments a community by setting its members apart from one another. In later chapters, we will consider more complicated attributes, such as intensity and cross-cutting, but these analyses will rest on the concept treated here: fragmentation (F).[1]

The central place given to fragmentation in this analysis is appropriate in light of its central place in politics itself. Where no cleavage produces any fragmentation whatever— an event which Madison rightly considered next to impossible— then the politics of a community are in an important sense trivial. There are no differences of trait, action, or opinion, and collective policies are apt to be a mere replication of individual policies. The political process, whereby the latter are aggregated to form public policy, amounts to nothing more than a sort of photography. In a sense, then, the degree of fragmentation produced by a cleavage suggests its importance for politics.[2] This is because it tells us how frequently members find themselves divided by the cleavage.

This extreme case, in which no fragmentation is produced by a cleavage, corresponds to a situation in which every pair of members crystallized by a cleavage contains persons from the same nominal group. That is, all pairs are matched, and none are mixed. Here, for ex-

1. The reader will recall that we are using "fragmentation" as a general term which subsumes "heterogeneity," "dissensus," and "fractionalization" as it applies to trait, opinion, and behavioral cleavages.

2. This is not to suggest that the cleavage's intensity does not also bear on the question. However, it is possible for a cleavage to produce an intense fragmentation only in so far as it produces extensive fragmentation. (F is theoretically prior to I.)

ample, we have racial cleavages in a one-race society, partisan cleavages in a one-party system, or opinion cleavages in a like-minded community. We have, then, cleavages which produce no fragmentation: to these, we assign a value of zero for F.

Consider, for the moment, an even more preposterous extreme in which every individual is set apart from every other by a given cleavage. The universe of pairs is now uniformly mixed: since every individual belongs to a distinct nominal group, every pair must be mixed. This, of course, constitutes the upper limit for fragmentation, to which our analysis assigns a value of unity. While plausible examples are hard to come by, this condition obtains in a committee in which each member considers himself the most desirable candidate for chairman. We have, then, the polar opposite of the unfragmented extreme outlined a moment ago.

Fragmentation varies in degrees between these hypothetical extremes. The problem before us is to find a way of assigning exact values to the degrees of fragmentation which lie between them and to give a useful theoretical interpretation for all these values. Let us proceed with the following steps: a definition of "cleavage," a definition of "crystallization," a purely formal definition of "fragmentation," a theoretical discussion of this definition, two computing formulae for fragmentation, and some applications to actual cleavages. A review of related literature is omitted here in favor of the catalogue appearing as Appendix A.

2.1 Definition of "Cleavage"

A cleavage is merely a division of a community—into religious groups, opinion groups, or voting groups, for example. "Formally, we define a "cleavage"as a family of sets of individuals. These sets might be called "groups" in the case of trait cleavages (e.g., religious groups) or "alternatives" in the cases of opinion and behavior cleavages (e.g., alternative opinions between which the individual chooses on some issue, or alternative political

24

parties between which he chooses when voting). The alternatives (or groups) are labeled A_1, A_2, . . . , A_n. It is assumed only that they are nominal groups. Let us suppose that the number of individuals committed to A_i is f_i, that the total number of individuals in the community is S, and that the number who actually choose an alternative is N. Then

$$\sum_{i=1}^{n} f_i = N$$

2.2 Definition of "Crystallization"

Not every cleavage touches every member of a community; often some members have no relevant opinion or make no relevant choice, leaving themselves outside the bounds of the cleavage. Our analysis of fragmentation concerns only that set of persons involved by the cleavage. We must, for this reason, have a way to indicate the extent to which the cleavage we are analyzing crystallizes the community. Let us define "crystallization" (C) as the proportion of a community which belongs to the set of persons crystallized by a cleavage.

$$C = \frac{N}{S}$$

C varies between 0 and 1. C = 1 when all persons are crystallized (N = S), and C = 0 when none are crystallized (N = 0), although we might say that the cleavage no longer exists when C reaches zero. Our analysis of fragmentation is confined to the crystallized part of the community. It will therefore be important that the value of C be given along with that for F (fragmentation) in every instance. The reader should assume that all sets of persons and of pairwise relations in the following discussion are confined to the elements of the crystallized community.

2.3 Formal Definition of "Fragmentation"

A perfectly fragmented community over some given cleavage has no matched pairs of individuals, since each individual belongs to his own nominal group. A perfectly unfragmented community has no mixed pairs of individuals who are divided by a cleavage, since all individuals belong to the same nominal group. Accordingly, we define "fragmentation (F)" as the proportion of all pairs of (crystallized) individuals which join members from different groups:

$$F = \frac{\text{number of mixed pairs}}{\text{total number of pairs}} \tag{2.1}$$

The total number of pairs from the N crystallized individuals is simply

$$\binom{N}{2} = \frac{1}{2} N (N - 1) \tag{2.2}$$

The number of mixed pairs (U, say) is the sum of the products of every frequency f_i with each other frequency f_j ($j \neq i$). So, for example, if we have three groups, containing 4, 3, and 2 persons each, the number of mixed pairs is $4 \cdot 3 + 4 \cdot 2 + 3 \cdot 2$, or 26. More formally, the number of mixed pairs (U) is

$$U = \sum_{i,j=1}^{n} f_i \cdot f_j \tag{2.3}$$
$$(j \neq i)$$

Substituting equations (2.2) and (2.3) in (2.1), we obtain

$$F = \frac{2}{N (N-1)} \sum_{i,j=1}^{n} f_i \cdot f_j \tag{2.4}$$
$$(j = i)$$

which is our formal definition of "fragmentation."

Let us illustrate this formula with a simple example. A hypothetical political committee has four Blacks, four Whites, and two Orientals: $f_1 = 4$, $f_2 = 4$, $f_3 = 2$. Since all ten persons have skins, crystallization is complete ($C = 1$), and $N = 10$. Using equation (2.4), we compute the fragmentation of this racial cleavage as follows:

$$F = \frac{2}{N(N-1)} (f_1f_2 + f_1f_3 + f_2f_3)$$

$$= \frac{2}{10 \cdot 9} (4 \cdot 4 + 4 \cdot 2 + 4 \cdot 2)$$

$$= \frac{64}{90} = .71$$

It will be seen from the definition of F given in equation (2.4) above that the bounds of F are 0 and 1. When the number of groups, n, is only 1, $F = 0$. When each individual is in a group by himself, so that $n = N$, then $F = 1$. In other cases the upper bound for F is found to be $N(n-1)/n(N-1)$ and is attained when the individuals are divided equally between the n groups (all f_i are equal). When N is large, so that $N/(N-1)$ is approximately 1, this upper bound is approximately $1 - 1/n$. For example, $F_{max} = .5$ when $n = 2$, and $F_{max} = .8$ when $n = 5$.

2.4 Interpretation

The values which this definition assigns to fragmentation have two simple and complementary interpretations. The first is based on the universe of pairs, and the second is based on a simple probability model. Let us discuss these interpretations, applying each interpretation to the racial cleavage in our example.

The universe of pairs

To speak of politics is to speak of interaction, of relationships between the members of a community. It is true that a political community consists of discrete individuals, but it is also true that the life of a community (qua community) is altogether relational. Men are men alone, but they are political actors only in and through their relationships with others. It follows that a cleavage is important not so much for what it says of individuals, but for what it says of their relationships with each other.

The simplest relationship joins two persons. Cleavage relations in larger groups, like the triad, are reducible to pairs of individuals, and what can be said of one triad can also be said of the three pairs which comprise it. What can be said of any crystallized community can also be said of the $1/2\,N(N-1)$ pairs which it contains. And, in a sense, it is more useful to speak of these $1/2\,N(N-1)$ pairs than of N individuals, for the individuals are part of the community only as they enter into relationships with one another.

For these reasons, it may be sensible to conceive the universe of pairs within a community as the web within which its political life occurs. These pairs are the potential arcs over which messages, bargains, and feelings may flow. They are the potential elements of action. And, for the political scientist, this web of pairs may be a useful screen on which to project the image of a cleavage system.

Consider table 2.1 and what it tells us about the life of our hypothetical committee. It suggests a nonwhite majority. This may be important, but in the present connection it is less important than the collateral information given by table 2.2. Table 2.2 gives us an account of the potential relationships between members in so far as race is significant. This new table gives information which was dormant in table 2.1. We may be surprised, for example, to find that more potential relations join Blacks with Whites (16) than join Blacks with Blacks (6) and Whites with Whites (6) put together, despite the equal number of Blacks and Whites. Table 2.2 is a projection of the racial cleavage onto the universe of pairs within which the committee's collective life occurs.

Table 2.3 is a condensation of this projection, which tells us how large a proportion of this universe is divided by race. It tells us how extensively race fragments the community. And this, we believe, is a parsimonious way to begin analyzing the racial cleavage's part in the life of the committee.

Table 2.1

Racial Composition of Committee
by Race

Individuals	Number
Black	4
White	4
Oriental	2

number of people (N) = 10

Table 2.2

Potential Relationships Between Committee Members
by Race

Pairs	Number
Black–Black	6
White–White	6
Oriental–Oriental	1
Black–White	16
Black–Oriental	8
White–Oriental	8

number of pairs = 45

Table 2.3

Potential Relationships Between Committee Members
by Racial Fragmentation

Pairs		Number
No. of Racially Matched Pairs (V)	=	13
No. of Racially Mixed Pairs (U)	=	32
		45

$$F = \frac{32}{45} = .71$$

We may pause here to formalize this way of understanding the values generated for fragmentation:

Conception of political community: A political community consists of the potential relationships between
its members. Its members are individuals, but its
constituent elements are pairs of individuals.
Interpretation of fragmentation: Fragmentation is the
proportion of a community so defined which is divided
by a cleavage. That is, fragmentation denotes the
number of elements divided by the cleavage as a
proportion of the total number of elements. [3]

In our example, the community has 10 members but
45 constituent elements, of which 71% are racially divided.
This is one way of interpreting the statement that F equals
.71.

Probability

A complementary interpretation is offered by a quite
simple probability model. Suppose we are interested in
the impact of the racial cleavage we have been considering on the day-to-day experiences of the committee's
members. We may be especially interested in the frequency with which members will interact with persons
whose skin is not the same color as their own. This might
interest us as a cue to levels of tension or as a measure
of racial integration. Given the random-interaction assumption about to be presented, we may evaluate fragmentation scores as the probability of encounters between
members of different nominal groups (i.e., races). In the
committee we have been considering, this probability
would be 0.71 — slightly more than a two-in-three chance
of racially mixed interactions.

3. Allowance must, of course, be made for uncrystallized
portions of communities, especially over behavioral and opinion
cleavages. "Community" here refers to the crystallized portion
of a population.

This interpretation requires the assumption that members interact randomly with each other. This means that each of the pairs is equally apt to be the basis of an actual encounter. This will, of course, almost never be the case; people always seek out some persons and avoid others. But the model-interpretation is not meant to be a description of reality so much as a template against which to silhouette realities.

Suppose, for example, that we were interested in the degree to which members of our illustrative community avoid or seek out mixed encounters. Observation tells us the proportion of actual encounters which are so mixed. The question then becomes, "What degree of avoidance or approach does this proportion represent?" The fragmentation value, coupled with this probabilistic interpretation, gives a convenient and relevant base line with which to compare empirically determined rates of mixed interaction. As these rates fall below .71, we have increasing reason to suspect that members avoid mixed encounters. As observed rates rise above this fragmentation value, we have increasing reason to suppose that the members seek out these encounters. The probability model serves in this instance as a useful basis of comparison; our comparisons tell us how apt the assumption of random interaction is to be incorrect, and this may (as in this case) be theoretically useful.

> Interpretation of fragmentation: Given the assumption of random interaction, fragmentation is the probability that mixed encounters will occur.

2.5 Computing Formulae

Our formal definition may be complete and direct; it is not, however, convenient. We pause here to introduce two computing formulae, one for small communities and one for large ones.

Computation for small n

The upper term in our definition requires that each frequency be cross-multiplied with every other term. It may, however, be useful to avoid this operation by computing the complement of F and subtracting this value from one.

The number of matched pairs in any nominal group A_i is $f_i(f_i - 1)/2$. Summing this over all groups and dividing by the total number of pairs, we obtain the proportion of all the pairs which are matched:

$$\frac{\frac{1}{2} \sum_{i=1}^{n} f_i(f_i - 1)}{\frac{1}{2} N(N - 1)}$$

We also know that all pairs which are not matched are mixed. Hence this quantity is the complement of F, and we have

$$F = 1 - \frac{1}{N(N-1)} \sum_{i=1}^{n} f_i(f_i - 1) \tag{2.5}$$

In our committee example

$$F = 1 - \frac{(4 \cdot 3) + (4 \cdot 3) + (2 \cdot 1)}{(10 \cdot 9)}$$

$$= 1 - \frac{26}{90}$$

$$= 1 - \frac{13}{45}$$

$$= \frac{32}{45}$$

$$= .71$$

This formula offers a modest economy of effort where a large number of nominal groups are encountered and where frequencies are not large enough to permit the approximation suggested below.

Computation for large N

Where we are considering very large numbers— thousands or millions— we may assume that

$$\frac{f_i(f_i - 1)}{N(N - 1)} \cong \frac{f_i^2}{N^2}$$

Using this approximation in equation (2.5), we have

$$F = 1 - \sum_{i=1}^{n} \left(\frac{f_i}{N}\right)^2 \tag{2.6}$$

where f_i/N is of course the proportion of individuals who are in A_i.

For very small numbers, like the ones used in our example, this computation vastly underestimates degrees of fragmentation. In the case of our ten-man committee, this approximation gives us a value of only .64 instead of .71:

$$F_{apx} = 1 - \left[\left(\frac{4}{10}\right)^2 + \left(\frac{4}{10}\right)^2 + \left(\frac{2}{10}\right)^2\right]$$

$$= 1 - \frac{36}{100}$$

$$= .64$$

This is an unacceptable error (.07 units of F). Suppose, however, that our committee contained 100 persons, in exactly the same proportions, producing frequencies of 40, 40, and 20. Then the correct value, under the exact formula in equation (2.5), would be 0.6465. Under the present approximation [using equation (2.6)], the value is

.6400. The error is now only 0.0065 units of F, which is for many purposes quite acceptable.

Let us turn now to some empirical applications which illustrate the uses (and abuses) of F.

2.6 Applications

The following pages offer two very different applications. In the first of these, fragmentation is used for strictly comparative purposes — to elucidate certain differences in religious diversity among western nations. Second, we offer an application of fragmentation in a theoretical context, in which the concept is used as a bridge between Madison's size-tyranny argument and certain contemporary actualities. These examples are meant to demonstrate the limitations, as well as the potentialities, associated with our conception of fragmentation.

A comparative application: religious heterogeneity

Fragmentation, as we said, is a formal concept which may be applied to any sort of cleavage. This means that its utility is quite general and is not limited to the class of cleavages which are ordinarily considered political. Nor, as we have also said, is its application limited to traits, to behaviors, or to opinions: fragmentation subsumes the concepts of heterogeneity, fractionalization, and dissensus which are associated with these three sources of cleavage.

This generality (as well as the formality by which it is achieved) gives us a great deal of theoretical flexibility, but it in no way alters the quality of the empirical information to be analyzed. No formal concept can be expected to make inaccurate data accurate. Moreover, any formal concept assumes that the analyst has made certain crucial decisions about the significance of data for the systems in which they are embedded. In order to illustrate these difficulties, we have chosen the perplexing example of religious cleavages.

Let us begin with the simple, often interesting question, "How greatly does religion fragment a given society?" And, as an immediate consequence, "How does this degree of fragmentation compare with that found in some other society?" Assuming that the "United Nations Demographic Yearbook" of 1956 is accurate, we may make one application of fragmentation and answer this question in one way. These answers are given by table 2.4, a table designed to point up the confusions which may arise from naïve faith in formal comparisons.

Table 2.4

Religious Fragmentation in Ten
Western Nations

Nation	F(Religion)
Netherlands	.64
West Germany	.54
Canada	.54
Switzerland	.50
Australia	.50
New Zealand	.39
Austria	.18
Ireland	.11
Luxembourg	.05
Norway	.02

Source: "United Nations Demographic Yearbook," 1956. Computed by equation (2.6).
Note: Crystallization (C) equals 1.0 in all cases, by convention (see text).

Missing from table 2.4 is any indication of the decisions made by the analyst about the significance of given religious divisions in given societies. The assumption which we made in producing the table was that three groups (and the three interfaces between them) are significant: Roman Catholic Christian, Protestant Christian, and non-Christian (including Jews, Buddhists, Moslems, and nonbelievers). This division may make sense for certain purposes and within certain classes of society, but it certainly is not sensible for all classes of questions and societies. It would, for example, show almost no fragmentation over religion in India.

The problem at hand may be called the definition of nominal groups, and there seem to be two broad strategies for coping with it. The simplest, reflected in table 2.4, is an a priori strategy in which the analyst decides on a definition of groups which he proceeds to apply universally. This strategy will be most useful when the kinds of nominal groups involved are the subject of well-defined and cross-culturally general definitions. This is the case with cleavage of electorates into political parties, for example. But, even within the set of nations compared in table 2.4, this a priori strategy raises genuine difficulties where religion is concerned.

For this reason, it may sometimes be more sensible to follow what we may call, for lack of a better term, an a posteriori strategy of definition. This might very well mean that the nominal groups decided upon for the various nations within the sample being compared will not be uniform. We might, in the case at hand, divide the Dutch so as to recognize the cleavage between Dutch and orthodox reform protestantism.[4] At the same time, we might treat the Protestants as a single group in certain other nations— perhaps Austria. And, for some purposes, we might say that these irregular definitions were of greater analytic utility than the relatively clean ones produced by an a priori definition strategy. The choice is a judgment which must be left to the analyst himself. For this reason, we suggest that an analyst who uses fragmentation (or any of the extensions offered below) be careful to define the nominal groups employed and to give some indication of the reasons for which he chose them.

4. See Lijphart 1968.

36

A theoretical application: Madison's size–diversity–tyranny argument

A very different use of our concept may be illustrated by executing a preliminary test of Madison's size–diversity–tyranny argument, in the manner proposed in chapter 1. We will see that fragmentation is crucial to the analysis and that failure to deal with the "diversity" terms it masters would have resulted in the most misguided conclusions. The reader should, of course, note that the aggregate data we have used in this analysis are in many ways imperfectly suited to the task, and that our conclusions must therefore be considered tentative. Nevertheless, the analysis illustrates the potential relevance of fragmentation to important theoretical issues, of which Madison's argument is an example.

As we said in chapter 1, Madison is defending a large republic (the U.S. as created by Constitution of 1787) in opposition to a collection of small republics (the states before the Constitution). Since his paramount concern was the avoidance of tyranny, Madison was left with the following proposition:

Proposition: Large republics are less subject to tyrannical policies than small ones.
Size = gross land area (variable A) and total population (variable P).
Tyranny = the percentage of the gross national product spent by the central government for purposes other than defense (variable T).

While this definition of tyranny is, in contemporary terms, preposterous, it is one indicator for what Madison had in mind. He was, after all, operating with a scale of values in which private property rights in particular, and economic freedom in general, held a very central place. He seems at least to have had economic deprivations in mind as one important example of tyranny. So, while variable T is not an exhaustive reckoning of what tyranny meant to Madison, it is probably one of the important things it did mean to him.

Now, if we leave aside the argument Madison gave for his assertion and focus only on the simple relations it entails, we arrive at a first test, using data for twenty contemporary republics as shown in table 2.5.[5] A casual inspection of tables lends plausibility to Madison's polemical assertion. The assertion leads us to expect a negative relationship between the two size variables on the one hand and the tyranny variable on the other. This appears in fig. 1.   All three correlations are significant at the .05 level (using a t-test with 18 degrees of freedom). So, putting aside the crudeness of the indicator we have chosen for tyranny, it must be supposed that Madison's assertion has some relevance to the contemporary world: the larger the republic, the lower the degree of tyranny.   At least the simple correlations point in that direction. This is as far as we can go without encountering diversity terms (and introducing "fragmentation").

It would, however, be a mistake to suppose that this first finding lends support to the theoretical argument with which Madison supports his assertion.   The assertion might be correct while the supporting argument was wholly or partly erroneous. We are now ready to use our concept of fragmentation to perform a preliminary test for the supporting argument itself.   We may do so by asking Madison what variables he thinks intervene between the variables of fig. 2.1, explaining the correlations between size and tyranny.   The answer, as we suggested in chapter 1, is shown in fig. 2.2.

5. The data in tables 2.5 and 2.6 were mostly taken from Russett et al. 1964 and completed using various issues of the "Statesman's Yearbook" and the "United Nations' Statistical Yearbook."   V and M were computed by ourselves.   The values of all the variables are those at 1960 or the closest date with available data.   In the case of V and M, the election of 1960 or the most recent election before 1960 was used. A fuller analysis might of course use some lagged variables in the analysis below.

Table 2.5

Raw Data for Madison Problem
(Time: About 1960)

	T Tyranny (%)	P Population (1000s)	A Area (1000 km².)	E Econ.	V Votes	M Majority Faction
1. Australia	13.70	10275	7,687	.822	.591	1
2. Austria	27.72	7048	84	.807	.597	0
3. Belgium	20.00	9153	31	.796	.642	0
4. Canada	11.40	17909	9,976	.829	.590	1
5. Denmark	15.20	4581	43	.806	.738	0
6. Finland	24.34	4430	337	.780	.807	0
7. France	14.60	45684	547	.821	.841	0
8. W. Germany	11.20	55423	249	.784	.721	0
9. Iceland	19.01	176	103	.776	.727	0

10. Ireland	24.48	2834	70	.783	.680	1
11. Israel	27.20	2114	21	.828	.802	0
12. Italy	15.40	49642	301	.806	.743	0
13. Luxembourg	22.50	314	3	.800	.701	0
14. Netherlands	17.10	11480	34	.803	.776	0
15. New Zealand	30.00	2372	269	.823	.579	1
16. Norway	15.10	3581	324	.822	.708	1
17. Sweden	21.00	7480	450	.792	.693	0
18. Switzerland	11.00	5362	41	.763	.810	0
19. U.K.	23.20	52508	244	.771	.561	1
20. U.S.	10.80	180684	9,364	.849	.500	1

40

Figure 2.1

Simple Correlations, Assertion Variables

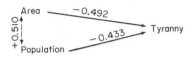

Figure 2.2

Linkage From Size Variables to Tyranny

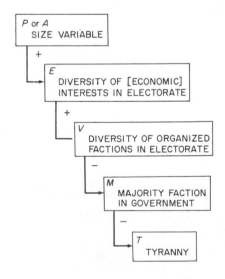

Two of the central variables (E and V) are what we have been calling diversity terms: they are concerned with degrees of fragmentation. With that in mind, we may supply the following operational interpretations of Madison's linking arument.

"Diversity of [Economic] Interests" = the fragmentation of the electorate over economic cleavages (variable E). We have used the International Labour Organization's standard sectors of the economy to define our nominal groups.[6]

"Diversity of Organized Factions" = the fragmentation of political parties, by votes (variable V).

"Majority Faction in Government" = the existence, or nonexistence, of a one-party majority in the lower house of the national legislature (variable M). We shall let M = 1 if there is a one-party majority and M = 0 otherwise.

The correlations between all seven variables are shown in table 2.6. Let us initially look only at those correlations associated with the links in the causal sequence suggested by Madison (fig. 2.2). First, we note that as size increases, so does economic diversity, as Madison argued; although one of these two relations (r_{PE}) is not quite significant at the .05 level. Moving to the second link, we see that r_{EV} is in the opposite direction to that hypothesized,

6. The first 9 sectors defined by the I.L.O. were used: (1) agriculture, forestry, hunting, and fishing; (2) mining and quarrying; (3) manufacturing; (4) construction; (5) electricity, gas, water, and sanitary services (i.e. the utilities); (6) commerce; (7) transport, storage and communication; (8) services; (9) activities not adequately described. The remaining 3 sectors (persons seeking employment for first time, armed forces, unemployed) have only a negligible effect on the value of E. We have used the approximate form of F for computation. See "Yearbook of Labor Statistics, 1965," International Labor Office (Geneva, 1966).

Table 2.6

Intercorrelations of All Seven Variables
(Correlations significant at the .05 level are underlined)

	A	P	E	V	M	T
A	1					
P	.510	1				
E	.590	.386	1			
V	−.581	−.417	−.343	1		
M	.573	.271	.369	−.699	1	
T	−.492	−.433	−.126	−.065	−.045	1

but it is found that this correlation is spurious, the "common cause" of these two variables being A. The partial correlation between E and V holding A constant (denoted as usual by $r_{EV \cdot A}$) is very close to zero, and we rule out the other possible interpretation that A intervenes between E and V.[7] This negative correlation between E and V, then, is due to that between A and V. This latter result is itself rather unexpected and is due to the fact that, out of the five countries which do not have a system of proportional representation (and hence have generally low V values), three— Australia, Canada, U.S.— have extremely large areas compared to the other countries. This is revealed in the positive (but insignificant) correlations which obtain between A and V and between E and V for the PR countries alone. The next link— the more or less trivial hypothesis that factional diversity works against one-party majorities— is confirmed ($r_{VM} = -.699$). Finally, the simple correlation between M and T is only −.045, but if we control for A (which is correlated .573 with M), then we find that $r_{MT \cdot A} = .35$, which is in the predicted direction. This effect is even stronger for the re-

7. Cf. Simon 1954.

lation between V and T: r_{VT} is only $-.065$, but $r_{VT \cdot A} = -.50$, which is significant and in the predicted direction. We can say, then, that if the value of A is held constant, Madison's hypothesis connecting tyranny with the existence of one-party majorities and the lack of factional diversity is not refuted.

Finally, we might ask, "What proportion of the variance of T is explained by the other five variables?" A linear regression of T on A, P, E, V, and M was performed, and the multiple regression coefficient was found to be $R = .755$. An analysis of variance (F-ratio based on 5 and 14 degrees of freedom) confirms that this regression is significant at the .05 level: the five independent variables significantly account for 57% ($R^2 = .570$) of the variance of T.[8]

Summarizing, it is reasonable to conclude that Madison's hypothesis is not refuted:

1. Tyranny decreases with size — the simple correlations r_{AT} and r_{PT} being negative and significant.
2. If we control for area, then tyranny decreases as factions become more diverse ($r_{VT \cdot A} = -.50$) and in the absence of a one-party majority ($r_{MT \cdot A} = .35$).
3. The variables A, P, E, and V (with or without M) significantly account for 57% of the variance of M.
4. The only simple correlations which are significant at the .05 level and not in the direction hypothesized by Madison are those involving V or M; this is quite possibly due to the effects of electoral laws.

One cannot be certain of what Madison really meant. He certainly did not have a multiple regression equation in mind when writing "Federalist 10"! But the analysis given here seems largely in keeping with the spirit of that essay; and if it is, then (within the limitations mentioned earlier) Madison's views are upheld. In any case, it has

8. If the variable M is omitted from this regression, then the value of R remains the same, but (with 4 and 15 degrees of freedom here) it is not significant as high as the .01 level.

not been our intention to explore this problem exhaustively, but rather to use it as an illustration of the utility of F as a measure of economic and political diversity.

2.7 Conclusions

In this chapter, we have presented the simplest unit of our analysis—fragmentation. We have shown that this concept offers a way of representing the degree to which a single cleavage sets the members of a community apart. The resulting values are, as we have suggested, subject to straightforward theoretical interpretations. And the concept may be applied to any kind of cleavage in any kind of community, once that community and the nominal groups comprising the cleavage are defined.

The concept of fragmentation is the kernel around which the remainder of this analysis is organized. But alone, fragmentation is far too simple to meet the complexities raised by the real world, or even by the less real world pictured in the existing literature. As things stand, we cannot represent the influence of variations in the intensities with which individuals cleave to their positions. And we cannot yet represent the intersection of cleavages—the degrees to which they overlap and cross-cut one another. In the chapters which follow, our analysis is extended to meet these difficulties.

CHAPTER 3: THE INTENSITY OF FRAGMENTATION

The concept of intensity has always been a central one in political science — above all for the democratic theorist concerned with the problem of intensity (for example, conflicts between intense minorities and apathetic majorities),[1] and, more generally, for any theorist of group decision-making concerned with the problem of aggregating individual preferences.[2] But it is also of considerable interest to the public opinion pollster, who has always known that knowledge of the intensity of an opinion as well as its direction is necessary for an accurate understanding of his poll,[3] and to the student of political behavior concerned with the implications of the distribution of intensities for political action.[4] In each of these areas (which are not, of course, distinct), there are problems requiring a precise definition of fragmentation (especially dissensus — in the case of opinion cleavages) which takes into account the intensity with which individuals cleave to their positions. This is the subject of the present chapter. But before we make use of intensities, let us be quite sure of what we mean by them.

3.1 The Concept of Intensity

"Intensity," it turns out, is a highly ambiguous word — a single word which stands as the surname for a whole

1. See, for example, Dahl 1956, chapter 4. In Kendall and Carey 1968, pp. 5-24, the intensity problem emerges not merely as "a special problem in the theory of populistic democracy," but "as a universal problem of politics."
2. For a lucid introduction to the problem and a discussion of intensities of preferences in that context, see Luce and Raiffa 1957.
3. See the early papers by Katz in Cantril 1944 (chapter 3); see also Cantril 1946, pp. 129-35.
4. See, for example, Key 1964, chapter 9; or Lane and Sears 1964, chapter 9.

family of concepts. If we use the word now as it has been used in the past, as though it had but one sense when in fact it has many, we would do little worse than we have sometimes done with other important terms such as "democracy," "power," or "representation." Wittgenstein believed that "what causes most of the trouble in philosophy is that we are tempted to describe the use of important odd-job words as though they were words with a regular function." It seems to us that this causes a great deal of trouble in political science, too. In the remainder of this section, then, we shall outline some of the major ambiguities in the concept of intensity which require clarification before we can proceed.

These ambiguities can be more easily explored if we concentrate our attention, for the time being, on particular problems. Thus, the following discussion will mainly concern the intensity problem in democratic theory: the aggregation of individual preferences to arrive at a public policy in such a way that justice (in some sense), or the future stability of the regime, is maximized.[5] In both these problems, the question arises of whether, in arriving at a public policy, individual preferences should be weighed in accordance with their intensity, and if so, how they should be weighed. Discussion of these problems will reveal ambiguities in "intensity" which must be taken into account in any use of the concept in political science, including the present study of cleavages.

Let us suppose we wish to describe the intensity of some single individual's preference in some single political choice. We need not worry whether he is a voter choosing among parties, a legislator choosing among bills, or an appointments committeeman choosing among nominees. We may label the alternatives from which he is to choose $A_1, A_2, \ldots, A_{n-1}$, and to these alternatives we may add one which corresponds to the status quo, calling it A_0. Now suppose it is said that this individual prefers A_1 with high (or not so high) intensity. The assumption

5. See especially Kendall and Carey 1968, and Dahl 1956.

that this statement is meaningful is implicit in a great many of the discussions of intensity in the literature of democratic theory; and it is quite explicit in many survey questions, where a respondent is simply asked to state how intensely he holds an opinion, or, having been asked to select an alternative (a policy or a candidate, for instance) which he prefers, he is further pressed to state how intensely he prefers that alternative. We shall see shortly that only in the special case when there are two choice alternatives available $(n = 2)$[6] does such a statement have a single natural meaning; otherwise it can be given several reasonable interpretations. However, this statement may serve, for the time being, as a model in the analysis of certain ambiguities raised by the term "intensity." We may ask three questions which will help to illuminate some of the statement's ambiguities:

1. Intensity compared to what?
2. Intensity compared to whom?
3. Intensity in what sense?

Let us look at these questions individually.

Intensity compared to what?

Intensity is an aspect of choice, and choice implies comparison.[7] If I choose A_1 with some degree of intensity, that intensity has to do with the difference between A_1 and some alternative to it (perhaps A_0). The sentence "I intensely prefer A_1!" is grammatically complete, but it makes sense analytically only if we add the phrase it implies—". . . to A_0." For simplicity, let us consider the example with which Professors Kendall and Carey intro-

6. We still use n to refer to the total number of alternatives. In this section, this includes the status quo.
7. The comparative basis of intensities is noted by Dahl 1956, chapter 4, who points out that wanting one alternative includes not wanting another alternative.

duce "intensity" in their discussion of the intensity problem in democratic theory.

> Dinner is over. Mr. and Mrs. Jones and Mr. and
> Mrs. Smith are having coffee. The question arises:
> What shall we do this evening? Play bridge? Go to
> the movies? Listen to some chamber music from the
> local FM station? Sit and chat? Each, in due course,
> expresses a "preference" among these four alterna-
> tives but with this difference: Mr. and Mrs. Jones and
> Mrs. Smith, though each has a preference, "don't much
> care." Their preferences are "mild" or "marginal."
> Not so Mr. Smith. His preference is "strong." He is
> tired, couldn't possibly get his mind on bridge, or
> muster the energies for going out to a movie. He has
> listened to chamber music all afternoon while working
> on an architectural problem, and couldn't bear any
> more. If the group does anything other than sit and
> chat, he at least will do it grudgingly. He "cares
> enormously" which alternative is chosen. [Kendall
> and Carey 1968, p. 5]

The alternatives, then, are as follows:

A_1: play bridge
A_2: go to a movie
A_3: listen to chamber music
A_4: just talk to each other
A_0: continued coffee-drinking

We are told that Smith intensely favors A_4, but it is
clear from the quotation above that his intensity arises
from at least three invidious comparisons: A_4-A_1, A_4-A_2,
and A_4-A_3. The argument is crucially simplified by the
fact that the three other alternatives Smith considers are
each about equally noxious to him. If, as would often be
the case, the three were not equally unacceptable to him,
then we would need a more specific interpretation of his
intensity. Each of the following understandings might be
applied to Smith's intense preference for A_4:

1. He intensely prefers A_4 to the next most attractive option (perhaps A_1, bridge).
2. He intensely prefers A_4 to the least attractive alternative (perhaps A_3, chamber music).
3. He intensely prefers A_4 to the alternative he thinks is most likely to be adopted if A_4 is rejected (perhaps A_2, a movie).
4. He intensely prefers A_4 to A_0, the status quo.

Analogous interpretations might of course be offered for the less intense preferences of his companions.

Thus, when there are n alternatives, including the status quo, the intensity of an individual preference for an alternative may involve any one of $n-1$ comparisons. In order to be unambiguous, any statement about such an individual's intensity must specify which of these comparisons is intended, except when there are only two alternatives before him. The two-alternative case is the only one which altogether avoids this difficulty. Professor Dahl, in A Preface to Democratic Theory (1956), did not expressly restrict his discussion of the intensity problem to the case of two alternatives, but all his examples do in fact involve only two alternatives. And the fortuitous circumstance that there are only two political parties in the United States has enabled many survey researchers to obtain and analyze meaningful data on intensities of party preferences without having to recognize this type of ambiguity. But we cannot rely upon a natural dualism in the world to save us from the possibility that three or more alternatives may appear.

When more than two alternatives appear, the necessity of multiple comparisons raises genuine theoretical problems. Kendall and Carey have discussed the ethical and stability problems in democratic theory as though only a single number is attached to an individual's preference intensity—as though there were only one intensity to be weighed. But let us suppose that, in order to maximize the stability of the regime, we wish to construct a decision rule which selects as the public policy that alternative which is, in some sense, most preferred by the society. We might begin by asking each individual how dissatisfied he would be if his most preferred alternatives were not adopted. If he wished to be clear in his response, he is quite likely to reply: "That would depend on which alternative is adopted." If his preference for A_1 (his most preferred alternative) over A_3 (his least preferred alternative) is very intense, whereas his preference for A_1 over A_2 is almost negligible, then he is likely to feel very dissatisfied if A_3 is adopted but quite happy with A_2. The consequences for regime stability are accordingly very different in the two cases. And his responses to a survey question asking him to state how intensely he preferred A_1 would be different, depending on whether he had in mind the (huge) difference between A_1 and A_3 or the (negligible) difference between A_1 and A_2.

Consider a much simplified example: members X and Y both express a very intense preference for A_1 (say, a general assessment on the town), and each is tacitly basing his intensity on the difference between A_1 and what he considers the worst possible alternative. But suppose that for X this worst possibility is a special assessment on his half of the town (A_2), while for Y this worst possibility is a similar levy on <u>his</u> half of the town (A_3). If A_2 is adopted, X may respond (violently, say) according to his expressed intensity. But if A_3 is adopted, his reaction will be quite different, because he now feels less intensely. Likewise, Y's intensity will have different values depending on whether A_2 or A_3 is adopted. For either the ethical analysis of majority rule or the analysis of regime stability, this multiple valuation of intensities will make a very great difference.

It seems, then, that we cannot usefully treat the majority-rule problem or the stability problem unless we take note of the intensities associated with all these comparisons. Except in the case of only two available alternatives, the decision rule in each case must "process" not merely the single ambiguous intensity attached to the most preferred alternative, as has been tacitly assumed by democratic theorists in the past, but the intensities associated with the comparisons between all pairs of alternatives.[8] For only then can it be known how much the adoption of an alternative will hurt an individual, for each possible alternative and for each individual. Clearly, such a refinement will greatly complicate any descriptive statement about intensities — but it will avoid a major ambiguity in our theories.

Before we leave this question, there is one other related difficulty we must mention. Consider again the explanation which Kendall and Carey (1968) offer for Mr. Smith's intense preference for A_4. He is intensely in favor of plain talk, we are told, mainly because he very much wishes to avoid the alternatives to it. But we might just as well suppose that he is intensely in favor of a chat for very different reasons. He might, say, be quite indifferent to bridge, a movie, or the music, but have a fantastic urge to talk unimpeded by these distractions. Intuitively, the difference between these bad-worse and good-better intensities seems important to us.

And there is at least some theoretical justification for the distinction. Suppose we are concerned with regime stability. We see that all the paired comparisons made by all the members of this regime show quite high intensity differences. How much need we fear for the life of the regime? Only if we set good-better and bad-worse comparisons apart in our analysis can we begin to guess. If most of these intense preferences are of the good-bet-

8. This assumes, of course, that we wish to take intensities into account at all, rather than merely using ordinal preferences. This point is briefly taken up again when we discuss the second type of ambiguity; a full discussion would be out of place here, for we are only concerned with the difficulties which would arise if intensities "are" to be used. We note, however, that the aggregation of ordinal preferences is fraught with considerable theoretical dangers, principally in connection with Arrow's Impossibility Theorem. See Arrow 1963; and, for a simple general discussion of these problems, Luce and Raiffa 1957, chapter 14.

ter variety, the threat to stability posed by a resolution of the issue seems remote. If, in contrast, most of the comparisons fall into the bad-worse class, the threat to stability may seem more immediate.

This distinction seems a little less urgent than the one discussed above, but we nevertheless think it may be worth keeping in mind. It does, unfortunately, raise some troublesome conceptual problems. It is less than obvious that we can establish a neat threshold between good-better and bad-worse comparisons. We might say that the former entail pairs of alternatives in which the rejected alternative would be chosen over the status quo (A_0) and the latter entail pairs in which the preferred alternative would not itself be preferred to the status quo. But is the status quo a useful anchorage? It would certainly be misleading if we used it where some people are quite pleased with things as they are and others are displeased with them. Suppose, to simplify the discussion, that each individual's preferences are transitive (i.e., if he prefers A_i to A_j and A_j to A_k, then he prefers A_i to A_k, for all i, j, k where $i \neq j \neq k$) and that, instead of describing an individual's preference intensities by associating an intensity number with every pair of alternatives, we associate a number directly with each alternative. This simply means that (for each individual separately) the alternatives can be positioned on a cardinal scale; the distances between any two alternatives on such a scale are measures of the intensity of an individual's preference for one over the other. Now, there is no reason why we should not represent disliked alternatives by negative numbers on this scale, letting the zero point (or origin) be the point of indifference — if one of the alternatives were positioned there, it would be neither liked nor disliked. [9] The point is that not only do all the intensity differences (distances between alternatives on the scale) have important consequences for stability but

9. The measures of intensity which have in fact been devised are strictly cardinal; i.e., they are unique only up to a linear transformation. Thus, they have an arbitrary origin and unit of measurement (see below).

that we must also know the absolute position of the pair of alternatives. Two equally-spaced alternatives may be both above the zero point, both below it, or separated by it; the consequences are different in each case.

Normally, however, different members will have different zero points—thus even if we could actually determine the zero point for each separate member, it would be of little use unless all the zero points were in some way comparable. The units of measurement of each intensity scale would also have to be comparable. This problem brings us to our next question.

Intensity compared to whom?

We have seen that, in considering either the ethical or the stability problems, we must know an individual's whole preference schedule before we can say what effect the adoption of each alternative will have upon him. It has tacitly been assumed that such information would be useful because, knowing the effect on each individual, we should be in a position to speak of the total effect of the adoption of each alternative. We have assumed, in other words, that preference intensities can be aggregated, and this is possible only if one individual's intensities can be compared with another's.

This assumption, in a weak form, has frequently been made in political science—for instance, in analyzing survey data on opinions, and the intensity with which they are held, by merely tabulating figures for the total number of persons at each level of intensity. The problem is present in a more acute form in democratic theory, since, as we have seen, whole sets of intensities must be compared. This problem—the interpersonal comparison of preference intensities (or utilities)—is hardly new, of course; it has been the object of a long controversy in economic theory. In this controversy there have been two issues, and they are both important to political theory: (1) Can interpersonal comparisons of preference intensities be made? (i.e., is there some operational procedure for establishing individual intensity scales in such a way that

54

they are comparable?) and (2) Do our theories even require cardinal measures of intensity, or can they be based upon simpler assumptions and concepts ("ordinal" preference, for instance) and still explain as much? Only a few brief comments are in order here.

Several procedures for obtaining cardinal measures of intensity and making interpersonal comparisons have been proposed but have not generally been acceptable.[10] A procedure first formulated by von Neumann and Morgenstern, based on the expected-utility hypothesis, is widely accepted as a means of constructing cardinal measures of intensity.[11] But it provides separate intensity scales for each individual, and since each of these scales is only unique up to a linear transformation, they cannot be compared interpersonally. Currently, then, no operational procedures which allow us to make interpersonal comparisons of intensity are available. But, as one economist writes, "It would be generally agreed, on the testimony of introspection and literature, and, as a matter of fact, on that of our daily behavior toward others, that persons can differentiate preference intensities." However, he goes on to say, "Whether this differentiation makes any difference is another question" (Rothenberg 1961, p. 137). This brings us to the second issue: do we need cardinal preference intensities at all? The answer currently given by most economists is that economic theory can do with-

10. Perhaps the best known of these are due to Armstrong 1951, and Goodman and Markowitz 1952. For a discussion and evaluation of these procedures and a comprehensive review of the whole controversy, see Rothenberg 1961, part 3. See also Luce and Raiffa 1957, pp. 345–53.

11. However, it too has many critics. As an empirical hypothesis, the expected-utility hypothesis has met with only partial success in the few experimental tests which have been conducted. See Rothenberg 1961, chapters 9, 10.

out them, in the sense that everything explained by the
earlier theories based upon cardinal utilities can also be
explained using only ordinal preferences.   Both of these
issues are extraordinarily important to political theory.
For if the economist's answer to the second question is
also true of political theory, then we have no need of the
concept of intensity.   And if it is found, after all, that at
least some aspects of politics are more accurately explained by the inclusion of intensities in our theories, then
not only must we know what we mean by "intensities," but
the meaning we attach to them must also make interpersonal comparisons possible.

The recent history of the utility concept in economic
theory should not, however, mislead us. The central importance of preferences among choice alternatives in
politics suggests that the intensity concept may play a
much more important role in political theory.   For instance, it is difficult to conceive of a realistic theory explaining regime stability in terms of political and social
cleavages, which does not (ultimately) need to take account
of the intensities with which individuals cleave to their
positions (their choices, their preferences).

Intensity in what sense?

People do not think of their own preference intensities
as neatly or uniformly as political scientists conceptualize
them. Indeed, the word "intensity" does not always play as
important a role in verbalizing the things we have been discussing as do other terms — "strength of feeling" and "in-
transigence," for example. Even when actors use the term
"intensity," they may well think of it very differently than
we do. This raises the problem of "verstehen" in social
science, put so well by Peter Winch:

> Although the reflective student of society, or of a
> particular mode of social life, may find it necessary
> to use concepts which are not taken from the forms
> of activity which he is investigating, but which are
> taken rather from the context of his own investiga-

tion, still these technical concepts of his will imply a previous understanding of those other concepts which belong to the activities under investigation. [Winch 1958, p. 89]

This is an important problem, one which may lead to theoretical difficulties. Consider again our respondent who announces his very intense preference for alternative A_1. Assume, further, that we have overcome the difficulties outlined above, so that we may specify the alternative our respondent is rejecting and overcome the formal problem of interpersonal comparison. Now, suppose that we begin making theoretical calculations without knowing anything more about this respondent and what political language means to him. The following are some things which might be intended by the announcement of this otherwise unambiguous strong preference.[12]

1. Allegiant-Subject's Usage: "If A_1 is adopted, I will be pleased (or advantaged); if not, I will be displeased (or disadvantaged). This is all I mean."

2. Allegiant-Participant's Usage: "If A_1 is not adopted, I will work very hard at getting it adopted later on." Or, "The price of my compliance with A_1 will be very high."

3. Alienated Participant's Usage: "If A_1 is not adopted, I will work very hard at getting the regime overturned."

Now, suppose we are interested in the problems of regime stability. Can we afford to treat these three illustrative usages interchangeably? Surely, we would not wish to draw the same inferences from answers 1 and 3. If, instead, we are interested in the ethic of majority rule, we will not want to enter these three answers identically

12. We have relied here on some of the vocabulary proposed by Almond and Verba 1965.

in our weighting system, because, for example, the second two responses do not have any direct ethical interpretations.

This suggests that intensity may not vary over any single continuum of the sort contemplated by Kendall and Carey (1968), or even over the ordination proposed by Dahl (1956). There may be nominal or qualitative breaks in the usages given to "intensity" and its near synonyms by different people. We may need, therefore, to subdivide the concept to take these qualitative differences into account. We might, for example, distinguish between passive, "subjectship" uses and active, "participantship" uses of the term. In any event, we had best be careful not to impose a conceptual unity where none exists.

Intensities and political cleavages

We have outlined three ways in which the apparently simple declaration that an individual prefers an alternative with some stated level of intensity is ambiguous and therefore theoretically troublesome. It has been shown that, strictly speaking, we cannot begin to enter an individual's reported intensity into our calculations until at least the following questions are answered:

1. What is the basis of his comparison? (Intensity compared to what?)

2. On what interpersonal scale are we to array his and others' intensities? (Intensity compared to whom?)

3. What general usage does he give to "intensity"? (Intensity in what sense?)

Any thinking we do about intensities and their implications will be very soft-headed indeed unless we begin with explicit resolutions of these ambiguities. These resolutions may necessarily be arbitrary in some senses, and they will certainly commit us to important limitations. We cannot hope, for example, to do any very exact thinking about intensity in general, for this is not at all one thing but a family of things. We must settle instead for analyses of intensity compared to what, compared to whom, and in what sense.

The results of our first discussion— intensity compared to what— do not imply that we must take into account all the preferences of each individual when defining fragmentation. We are limiting ourselves throughout to the case where each individual chooses only one alternative.[13] In opinion cleavages, this would normally be his most preferred alternative, and a ranking (or paired comparisons) of all the alternatives would be possible. In most trait and behavioral cleavages, a ranking would not be possible: a person belongs to only one group, or he has taken (or can take) only one action. But in all three types of cleavage, the first type of ambiguity in the intensity concept is relevant: the individual chooses only one alternative (so that we are concerned with the intensity of only one preference), but the intensity of his preference will depend upon which other alternative he uses as his basis of comparison. In defining the "intensity of fragmentation" (I), we now appear to be faced with an embarrassing complexity: if there are n alternatives, then instead of there being only one intensity attached to each individual's choice, there are $n-1$ such intensities, corresponding to comparisons with the other $n-1$ alternatives. In a particular investigation, however, it might be sufficient to use only the intensity corresponding to one specified comparison— for example, that between the most preferred and the least preferred alternatives.[14] Of course, for a complete description of the intensity of fragmentation, one could calculate I for each of the $n-1$ possible comparisons (first using the intensity

13. Except in Appendix B, where we briefly review some measures of consensus among whole preference schedules, i.e., rankings of all the alternatives.

14. In a theoretical investigation, this simply means that "intensity" could be defined in terms of this one comparison. In an empirical investigation, the data would have to be gathered with reference to this comparison, e.g., by asking each respondent to state the intensity with which he prefers his choice over his least preferred alternative.

obtained from the comparison with the second most preferred alternative, then using the intensity of preference
over the third most preferred alternative, and so on), con-
ceivably redefining the intensity of fragmentation as the
mean of these n−1 I's. Here we shall simply define one I.
but it should be remembered that it is defined in terms of
intensities which are associated with one specific comparison. We shall therefore speak of only one intensity.
The same analysis could be given for each of n−1 intensities.

It has been pointed out that currently there exist no
procedures for measuring the intensities of different individuals on the same scale. Clearly, we cannot begin to
solve the problem of interpersonal comparisons in this
brief monograph. But the problem is present here in a
weak form: we do not ask each individual to array all the
alternatives along an intensity scale, but only to select
one alternative and state his intensity of preference for
that alternative. Such intensities will perhaps be more
comparable if the scale is fixed in advance and each individual is either asked to select a point on the scale or
is assigned to one.[15] We shall assume that these intensities are "measured" at the ordinal level—i.e., they can
be ordered. We label the intensity ranks R_1, R_2, . . . , R_m
in order of increasing intensity. This, of course, does not
solve the problem of interpersonal comparisons, since two
individuals may both state that they prefer an alternative
"very strongly" (the highest available intensity rank, say),
but one may in fact feel more intensely than the other.

With respect to the third ambiguity in the intensity
concept, the only practical precaution which can be taken
is to ensure that the intended sense of intensity (or which-
ever word is used) is explicit in the question used, or in
the procedure used to assign a person to an intensity rank.

15. This is, of course, what is done in most surveys, when
an individual is first asked for his opinion (i.e., to choose one
of n alternatives) and then asked how intensely he holds the
opinion ("very strongly," "strongly," etc.).

In what follows, we assume that intensities are comparable in this sense. Our analysis recognizes but does not resolve the intrinsic ambiguities of intensity as a theoretical concept.

Intensities and alternatives

Very frequently, in discussions of cleavage and intensity and of opinion distributions generally, intensities are themselves conceived as alternatives, and these intensities are assumed to be ordered. Suppose, for example, that each respondent in a survey is asked how he feels about some statement— whether he agrees strongly, agrees but not very strongly, is indifferent, disagrees but not very strongly, or disagrees strongly. In analyzing such data, one would either view agreement and disagreement as two (nominal) alternatives, indifference as a third alternative, and "strongly" and "not very strongly" as two intensity ranks; or view the five possible responses as five alternatives (with no intensities) and assume one ordering, based on degrees of agreement. Our own feeling is that it is difficult to justify the second view and that, as far as implications for subsequent political action are concerned, an important feature of such data is the existence of two distinct (nominal) groups— those for and those against. Under the assumption of one ordering of all the degrees of agreement and disagreement, the political importance of this dichotomy is lost. Consider a more specific example. In the national survey conducted by the Survey Research Center before the 1952 election, respondents were classified as supporting one of the two political parties or neither party. Supporters of Eisenhower or Stevenson were then asked, "Do you think it would make a good deal of difference to the country whether the Democrats or the Republicans win the election— or that it won't make much difference which side wins?" The possible responses were (A) "good deal of difference," (B) "some difference, minor difference," and (C) "no difference." The results are shown in fig. 3.1.[16]

16. These data are from Campbell, Gurin, and Miller 1954, p. 38. Figure 3.1 is taken from Dahl 1956, p. 95.

Figure 3.1

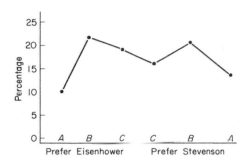

Again, it is possible to view these six responses as ordered alternatives, as indicated in fig. 3.1, but the assumption of ordinality for this type of data appears to us to be highly questionable. The assumption is essentially that there exists an underlying unidimensional scale on which the six alternatives shown on fig. 3.1 can be located. This means, in the present example, that the more one likes Stevenson, the less one likes Eisenhower—a very strong assumption. And as in the first example, the important division here (in its implications for party competition and the outcome of the election, for instance) is between two nominal alternatives (Eisenhower, Stevenson), not between six ordered alternatives. The view taken here, then, is that the Eisenhower supporters and the Stevenson supporters constitute two nominal groups, with A, B, and C as three intensity ranks in each group. [17]

17. Data on intensities have themselves been used, in connection with Guttman scales, to study the problem of whether the two ends of an attitude scale are in some sense opposite. The data for Guttman's scalogram analysis consist of the individual's responses to several questionnaire items, each of which attempts to tap the same underlying attitude. Each item has several possible alternative responses which are ordered on the hypothesized attitude continuum. The problem in scalogram analysis is that of testing whether the continuum defined

Figure 3.2

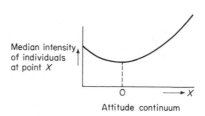

Attitude continuum

by each of the items is the same one. If it is, then the attitude
is said to be "scalable"; that is, there exists an underlying one-
dimensional continuum on which the individuals can be ranked
in order of the degree to which they possess the underlying attitude. If the data furnish a scale, we can say that one individual
is (for instance) more favorable than another, but the question
then arises of whether we can fix a cutting point, or origin, on
the continuum which divides the individuals into those favorable
and those unfavorable. This is the same as asking if the two
ends of the continuum are opposites in some sense, a question
which is of obvious importance in many political contexts such
as the study of political ideology, party competition, and conflict.
Stouffer and his associates found that, for a large number of
attitude areas, average intensity increased with the extremity
of the attitude position, so that the curve of intensity against
scale position is approximately U-shaped, as shown in fig. 3.2.
Assuming this relationship to hold, the required cutting point,
or origin, was taken as the point on the attitude continuum (point
0 in fig. 3.2) corresponding to the lowest point on the intensity
curve.

For full details of this work, the reader should consult
Stouffer et al. 1950, chapter 7. For discussions of scalogram
analysis, with numerous examples, see Stouffer, chapters 1, 3,
5, 6, 7, 8, and Coombs 1964, chapter 11. It should be remembered that the U-curve result was reported only in connection
with Guttman scales. Several examples of such U-curves are
given in Stouffer, chapter 7.

3.2 A Measure of the Intensity of Fragmentation

In chapter 2 we divided the set of all pairs of the N individuals in the crystallized portion of the community into matched pairs and mixed pairs. A matched pair was one in which both members were in the same groups, and, in chapter 2, extent of fragmentation (F) was defined as the proportion of all pairs which are matched pairs. The remaining pairs were mixed—a mixed pair being one whose two members were in different groups. These mixed pairs are the basis for the measure of intensity of fragmentation, which will now be developed.

Formally, we are given n alternatives, A_1, A_2, . . . , A_n, with corresponding frequencies f_1, f_2, . . . , f_n. No assumptions are made about the ordering of these alternatives; they are merely nominal alternatives. Within each alternative, the individuals are distributed over m intensity ranks, R_1, R_2, . . . , R_m(in order of increasing intensity). It may be helpful to picture the alternatives, or groups, as they are shown in fig. 3.3. Here there arc four groups (n = 4), and three intensity ranks (m = 3); the groups are represented by the "arms," and the intensity ranks are numbered outward (with increasing intensity) along the arms. It should be remembered that the cyclical order of the arms is totally arbitrary. We denote by f_{ij} the number of individuals at rank R_i of group A_j. These frequencies are also indicated in fig. 3.3.

	A_1	A_2	. . .	A_j	. . .	A_n
R_1	f_{11}	f_{12}	. . .	.	. . .	f_{1n}
R_2	f_{21}	f_{22}	. . .	.	. . .	f_{2n}
.	.	.	. . .	.	. . .	.
R_i	.	.	. . .	f_{ij}	. . .	.
.	.	.	. . .	.	. . .	.
R_m	f_{m1}	f_{m2}	. . .	.	. . .	f_{mn}

A more convenient representation of the frequencies is obtained by defining a matrix (f_{ij}), whose rows correspond to the intensity ranks R_i and whose columns correspond to the alternatives A_i. The total set of data thus consist of the crystallization (C) and the above matrix. The number of individuals f_j who are in group A_j is, of course, the jth column sum of the matrix—that is

$$f_j = \sum_{i=1}^{m} f_{ij}$$

Figure 3.3

Distribution of Choices Over Three Intensity Ranks
(m = 3) on Four Alternatives (n = 4)

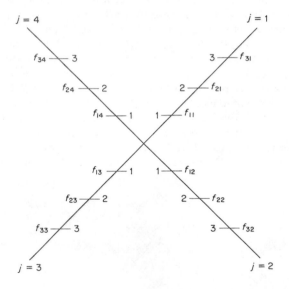

The "distance" (d) between two members of a mixed pair is defined as the number of intensity ranks between them; more formally, we define the distance between an individual at rank i_1 and an individual (in a different group) at rank i_2 as

$$d = (i_1 - 1) + (i_2 - 1)$$
$$= i_1 + i_2 - 2$$

Thus, for example, the distance between two individuals, each at rank 1 but in different groups, is zero; and the distance between an individual at rank 2 in group 1 (i.e., contributing to f_{21}) and an individual at rank 3 in group 3 (i.e., contributing to f_{33}) is 3. Thus d can be thought of as an "intensity distance." It may assume integer values from 0 through $2m - 2$.

It is important to note that labeling the ranks with integers and defining d as an arithmetic operation on these integers does not strictly imply that the intensity ranks can be measured in any way, or even that the intervals between the ranks can be measured. The use of the integers here and the definition of d are quite legitimate, since an intensity rank number such as i is, strictly speaking, the number of ranks from the center, and arithmetic operations may be performed on these numbers. The distinction here is between counting and measurement, and we are dealing with the former. For example, d is merely the number of ranks separating two individuals; it is not an interval level measure of distance. Thus, the formal derivation of the measure of intensity of fragmentation (I) given below requires only the assumption of ordinality of the intensity ranks. However, as we shall see, our definition of I will have a more intuitively reasonable interpretation if the intervals between the ranks are approximately equal.

We now consider, as our basis for measuring I, the proportions (P_d) of mixed pairs whose two members are a distance d apart, for each possible value of d ($d = 0, 1, 2, \ldots, 2m-2$). We define

$$P_d = \frac{\text{number of mixed pairs whose two members are exactly d apart}}{\text{total number of mixed pairs}}$$

Clearly, if all the individuals are at the most extreme intensity rank (R_m), then, no matter what the distribution between groups, the intensity of fragmentation should be at a maximum; that is, I must be defined so that it attains its maximum value for this extreme case. From the above definition of P_d, we see that in this case

$P_d = 1$ for $d = 2m-2$ (the maximum value of d)

$\quad = 0$ for all other values of d

The other extreme is the distribution in which all the individuals are located at the lowest intensity rank (R_1) in each group. Intensity of fragmentation should then be at a minimum. We see that in this case

$P_d = 1$ for $d = 0$ (the minimum value of d)

$\quad = 0$ for all other values of d

Thus, as the distribution of individuals over the intensity ranks varies between these two extremes, I will vary between its minimum value and its maximum value.

In the first place, we shall derive a general expression for P_d in terms of the frequencies f_{ij}. The set of values of P_d (for $d = 0, 1, \ldots, 2m-2$) can be thought of as a distribution of the mixed pairs over subsets defined by the various intensity distances; and we have

$$\sum_{d=0}^{2m-2} P_d = 1$$

This P_d distribution is a measure of the intensity of fragmentation: the more it is skewed toward high values of d, the more intensity there is. It is desirable, though, to have a measure consisting of a single number, and so we shall later combine the P_d's to form a single index I.

Derivation of P_d

The total number of pairs, matched or mixed, is $\binom{N}{2}$, or $N(N-1)/2$, where N is the total number of individuals in the crystallized portion of the community. Of these pairs, there are

$$U = \frac{1}{2} \sum_{\substack{i,j=1 \\ (j \neq i)}}^{n} f_i \cdot f_j$$

pairs which are mixed, where f_i is the frequency corresponding to alternative A_i. Another expression for this is obtained as follows. The proportion of pairs which are mixed is F, where F is the extent of fragmentation. Thus, the number of mixed pairs is $U = FN(N-1)/2$. We must now determine what proportion of these pairs are a distance d apart, for each value of d.[18]

Consider a typical mixed pair. Suppose one member of the pair is at the i_1^{th} intensity rank of the jth group, and the other member is at the i_2^{th} rank of the kth group, with $k \neq j$. The number of such pairs is $f_{i_1 j} \cdot f_{i_2 k}$, and they form a proportion of all the mixed pairs of

$$\frac{f_{i_1 j} \cdot f_{i_2 k}}{U} \tag{3.1}$$

Suppose that these two individuals are a distance d apart. Then, since $d = i_1 + i_2 - 2$, we have $i_2 = d + 2 - i_1$, so that expression (3.1) becomes

$$\frac{f_{i_1 j} \cdot f_{d+2-1,k}}{U} \tag{3.2}$$

The P_d's will be sums of terms like expression (3.2); the problem is to derive a general expression which will specify over which values of i_1, j, and k the summation must be made for given values of m, n, and d.

18. Reference to a diagram like that of fig. 3.3 may help the reader to follow the remainder of this derivation.

It is clear that the summation must be performed over all possible pairs j,k for k ≠ j — each pair corresponding to a different pair of groups A_j, A_k. Replacing i_1 in expression (3.2) by t, we thus have

$$P_d = \frac{1}{2U} \sum_{\substack{j,k=1 \\ (k \neq j)}}^{n} \sum_t f_{tj} \cdot f_{d+2-t,k} \qquad (3.3)$$

The 2 now appears in the denominator of equation (3.3) since the summation over all j and k counts each mixed pair twice, once for the two orderings of the pair's members.[19]

We now require general expressions for the upper and lower bounds for the t-summation.[20] Since we wish to sum over all possible pairs of individuals separated by d, t would run up to t = d + 1, provided that d + 1 ≤ m; this is, of course, not always the case, since the maximum value of d is 2m − 2. Thus, in general, the upper bound in the t-summation is the minimum of the pair (d + 1, m). For values of d less than or equal to m, the summation over t will clearly start at t = 1. But for d ≥ m, no pair of individuals separated by d can have one of the individuals

19. If the P_d's were being computed manually, then each mixed pair would be counted only once, and it would not be necessary to divide by 2, as in equation (3.3). But in writing out the general formula for P_d, it is more convenient to use the form of summation for (j,k) which we have used in equation (3.3). For simplicity, then, this form (necessitating the 2 in the denominator) will be used throughout.

20. The reader may not wish to follow this argument, since it is a simple matter, especially using a diagram like that of fig. 3.3, to perform this summation for a given set of data by picking out all those pairs of notches on the diagram which are separated by a distance d, for each value of d. But the derivation of a general formula for P_d is necessary if we are to examine the properties of the P_d's (and hence, of the measure of intensity of fragmentation to be proposed below). Furthermore, the computation by hand of all the P_d's, if m is not very small, is extremely tedious, while it is a simple matter to write a short computer program to find them. For this, though, it is necessary to formulate a general expression for P_d.

at a first rank (R_1); in fact, the lowest possible rank for either of the two individuals is $t = d + 2 - m$ (for $d \geq m$). For example, if $m = 2$ (the lowest value of m), this minimum value of t is equal to d; so that the t-summation for P_d must start at $t = 2$. (The summation for P_1 starts at $t = 1$, since $d + 1 \leq m$ in that case.) In the case $m = 3$, we have the following: for P_1 and P_2 the t-summation starts at $t = 1$; for $d > 2$ it starts at $t = d + 2 - m = d - 1$, that is, at $t = 2$ for P_3 and at $t = 3$ for P_4. Of course, the largest possible value of d here is 4.

Thus, in general, the t-summation runs from the maximum of the pair $(1, d + 2 - m)$. Inserting these bounds on the t-summation in equation (3.3), we finally have

$$P_d = \frac{1}{2U} \sum_{\substack{j,k=1 \\ (k \neq j)}}^{n} \sum_{\substack{t=max \\ (1,d+2-m)}}^{min(d+1,m)} f_{tj} f_{d+2-t,k} \tag{3.4}$$

We note that, if N is small, the P_d's are highly dependent on the values of N. For large values of N, this dependence is negligible, and the formulae will give highly accurate results if the f_{ij}'s are interpreted as proportions (of the total number of individuals, N). This requires, of course, that $N(N-1)$ be omitted from the denominator of equation (3.4), i.e., that 2U be replaced by F. This approximation is analogous to the one made in chapter 2.

All the P_d's can be calculated from equation (3.4); finally, for each value of d in turn, the appropriate frequencies are substituted from the (f_{ij}) matrix. Using equation (3.4), then, we can calculate the proportions of all mixed pairs whose members are separated by distances of $0, 1, 2, \ldots, 2m-2$; and this gives an initial indication of the intensity of fragmentation, I. Before defining I in terms of the P_d's and discussing its properties, we first give a detailed example, to show the use of the formula given by equation (3.4).[21]

21. The proportions P_d can, of course, be thought of in probability terms. In fact, P_d, as defined by equation (3.4) above, is equal to the probability that two individuals, drawn at random (without replacement of the first-drawn individual) from the crystallized portion of the community, are separated by an intensity distance d.

An example

We may illustrate our calculations by considering the responses which Albert Somit and Joseph Tannenhaus elicited from a sample of American political scientists by the sentence, "The really significant problems of political life cannot be successfully attacked by the behavioral approach."[22] Let A_1 represent the group agreeing with the statement and A_2 represent the group dissenting from it, and let R_1 be the intensity rank for mere agreement or disagreement and R_2 the rank for strong responses. We obtain the following matrix:

$$
\begin{array}{cc}
 & A_1 \qquad A_2 \\
\begin{array}{c} R_1 \\ R_2 \end{array} &
\begin{bmatrix} 241 & 318 \\ 144 & 139 \end{bmatrix}
\qquad \begin{array}{l} C = .84 \\ N = 842 \end{array} \\
 & 385 \qquad 457
\end{array}
$$

Here, m and n are both small—m = 2, n = 2—and d can take only the values 0, 1, 2. The extent of fragmentation F was found to be .49694. Using either of the two formulae, the number of mixed pairs U is 175,945. Thus the denominator term in equation (3.4) is 2U = 351,890.

Substituting in equation (3.4) for n and m, we have, for d = 0

$$
P_0 = \frac{1}{351890} \sum_{\substack{j,k=1 \\ (k \neq j)}}^{2} \sum_{t=1}^{1} f_{tj} f_{2-t,k}
$$

$$
= \frac{1}{351890} \sum_{\substack{j,k=1 \\ (k \neq j)}}^{2} f_{1j} f_{1k}
$$

$$
= \frac{1}{351890} \left(f_{11} f_{12} + f_{12} f_{11} \right)
$$

22. Somit and Tannenhaus 1967. See section 1.2:1 for the details.

Substituting for f_{11} and f_{12} from the matrix, we find

$P_0 = .4356$

Similarly, for $d = 1$

$$P_1 = \frac{1}{351890} \sum_{\substack{j,k=1 \\ (k \neq j)}}^{2} \sum_{t=1}^{2} f_{tj} \, f_{3-t,k}$$

$$= \frac{1}{351890} \sum_{\substack{j,k=1 \\ (k \neq j)}}^{2} (f_{1j} \, f_{2k} + f_{2j} \, f_{1k})$$

$$= \frac{2(f_{11} f_{22} + f_{21} f_{12})}{.351890}$$

$$= .4507$$

Finally, for $d = 2$, we find

$$P_2 = \frac{2(f_{21} f_{22})}{351890}$$

$$= .1138$$

Thus, the distribution of the mixed pairs over the intensity distances, i.e., the P_d's, is as follows:

	$d = 0$	$d = 1$	$d = 2$
$P_d =$	.4356	.4507	.1138

We noted earlier that the P_d's should always sum to unity; that is

$$\sum_{d=0}^{2m-2} P_d = 1$$

It will be seen that this is in fact the case for the results obtained in this example—a check on our calculations.

Definition of "intensity of fragmentation"

We wish to define the "intensity of fragmentation" (I) in such a way that I is large when the P_d distribution is skewed toward the high values of d, reaching a maximum when $P_{2m-2} = 1$ and $P_d = 0$ for $d \neq 2m-2$, and is small when the P_d distribution is skewed toward the low values of d, reaching a minimum when $P_0 = 1$ and $P_d = 0$ for $d \neq 0$. The simplest measure for I which satisfies these criteria is a weighted sum of the P_d's, each P_d being weighted by the corresponding intensity distance d. Thus, we define the intensity of fragmentation as

$$I = \frac{1}{2m-2} \sum_{d=0}^{2m-2} dP_d \tag{3.5}$$

$(2m - 2)$ being the maximum value of

$$\sum_{d=0}^{2m-2} dP_d$$

which arises when all the individuals are at the highest intensity rank (R_m), so that $P_{2m-2} = 1$ and $P_d = 0$ for $d \neq 2m - 2$.[23]

23. I can, of course, be expressed directly in terms of the frequencies f_{ij}. Substituting for P_d from equation (3.4) into equation (3.5), we have

$$I = \frac{1}{2m-2} \sum_{d=0}^{2m-2} \frac{d}{2U} \sum_{\substack{j,k=1 \\ (k \neq j)}}^{n} \sum_{t} f_{tj} f_{d+2-t,k}$$

$$= \frac{1}{(2m-2)\,2U} \sum_{d} \sum_{j,k} \sum_{t} [d \cdot f_{tj} f_{d+2-t,k}]$$

in which it can be clearly seen how the contribution to I of each mixed pair, whose members are a distance d apart, is weighted by the distance d. I, then, is simply a generalization of F, in that it is a form of weighted pairwise disagreement, the weights corresponding to intensity distances.

The choice of this weighting scheme may appear to be arbitrary. Therefore, we shall later take a geometrical and more intuitive approach to the definition of I— but we shall nevertheless arrive at the same measure as the one above. We note here that the only assumption about the intensity ranks which is required in the formal derivation of I is that they are ordered. This is so, we recall, because the distance d is arrived at by counting rather than by any process of measurement. However, when defined as a sum of weighted P_d's, I will correspond to our intuitive notions of intensity of fragmentation only if the intervals between the intensity ranks are approximately equal.

If only the value of I is required, it is not necessary to calculate P_0, as it contributes nothing to I. This, incidentally, does not mean that I does not use all the information contained in the P_d distribution— since

$$\sum_{d=0}^{2m-2} P_d = 1$$

the value of P_0 is implied by the values of P_1, P_2, ... , P_{2m-2}. However, deriving all the P_d's from the formula affords a check on our calculations.

It will now be shown that I has the properties mentioned above. First, I will be a minimum for the extreme distribution in which there are only individuals at the low-intensity rank (R_1), no matter what the distribution between groups. In this case, $P_0 = 1$, and $P_d = 0$ for $d \neq 0$. This follows immediately from the definition of P_d as noted earlier. It also follows from the formula for P_d in equation (3.3), by substituting $f_{ij} = 0$ for all $i \neq 1$ and for all j. Substituting these values for the P_d's in equation (3.5), we have $I_{min} = 0$. Next, the maximum value of I occurs when all individuals are at the most extreme intensity rank (R_m), no matter what the distribution between groups. Here, $P_d = 0$ for $d \neq 2m - 2$, and $P_{2m-2} = 1$. Again, this follows immediately from the definition of P_d, or from the formula in equation (3.3), by substituting $f_{ij} = 0$ for all $i \neq m$ and for all j. Substituting these P_d values in equation (3.5), we have $I_{max} = 1$. Thus, I varies between zero and one.

A geometric derivation of "I"

We shall now require the "cumulated" distribution of the P_d's. This is defined as follows:

$$CP_d = \sum_{i \geq d} P_d \text{ for each value of } d = 0, 1, \ldots, 2m-2$$

Notice that this is not quite the usual cumulated distribution. Instead, the cumulation is backward; that is, the P_d's are cumulated in the direction of decreasing d. Thus, CP_d is the proportion of mixed pairs whose members are separated by a distance of d or more.

Consider the following two hypothetical P_d distributions (where the value of m is 3):

		d = 0	d = 1	d = 2	d = 3	d = 4
P_d	A	.40	.25	.15	.10	.10
	B	.10	.15	.25	.30	.20

The curves[24] for these distributions are shown in fig. 3.4. We see that distribution A is skewed toward the low values of d, and distribution B toward the high values. Clearly, there is greater intensity of fragmentation in B than in A. In fact, from equation (3.5) we find that

for distribution A: I = .3125
for distribution B: I = .5875

Now consider the cumulated distributions. The CP_d's for these two distributions are found to be as follows:

		d = 0	d = 1	d = 2	d = 3	d = 4
CP_d	A	1.0	.60	.35	.20	.10
	B	1.0	.90	.75	.50	.20

24. Such curves are, of course, histograms. The P_d distribution is discrete, as is the CP_d distribution. This fact should be borne in mind later when we calculate areas under CP_d curves.

Figure 3.4

Two Hypothetical P_d Distributions

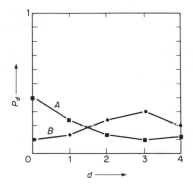

Figure 3.5

CP_d Distributions for the P_d Curves in Fig. 3.4

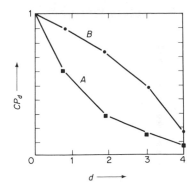

The CP_d curves are shown in fig. 3.5. We notice immediately that B bulges farther away from the d-axis than A. Indeed, it can be shown that the greater the value of I under the previous definition, given by equation (3.5), the greater the area under the corresponding CP_d curve. We therefore tentatively identify the intensity of fragmentation with this area.

Consider the two extreme cases. From the P_d distribution for the cases of minimum I and maximum I given above, we obtain the following results for the CP_d's:

I_{min}: $CP_d = 1$ for $d = 0$

$\quad\quad\quad = 0$ for $d \neq 0$

I_{max}: $CP_d = 1$ for all d

Two CP_d curves for these distributions are shown in figs. 3.6 and 3.7; they are drawn as histograms. Thus, the area under the CP_d curve is at its minimum for I_{min} and at its maximum for I_{max}. Since we do not wish P_0 to contribute to the intensity of fragmentation, we consider only the area under the CP_d curve for $d \geq 1$. Then, the minimum area is zero and the maximum area is $(2m-2) \cdot 1$.

Figure 3.6

CP_d Histogram for minimum I

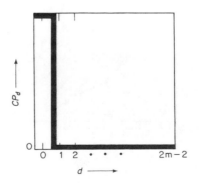

Figure 3.7

CP_d Histogram for maximum I

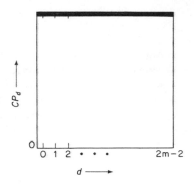

We now define "intensity of fragmentation" as

$$I' = \frac{\text{area under } CP_d \text{ curve}}{\text{maximum possible area}}$$

Thus, remembering the method of cumulating the P_d's, we have

$$I' = \frac{CP_1 + CP_2 + \ldots + CP_{2m-2}}{2m - 2}$$

$$= \frac{1}{2m - 2} \left[(P_1 + P_2 + \ldots + P_{2m-2}) + \right.$$
$$(P_2 + P_3 + \ldots + P_{2m-2}) +$$
$$\left. \ldots + (P_{2m-3} + P_{2m-2}) + (P_{2m-2}) \right]$$

$$= \frac{1}{2m - 2} \left[(2m - 2) \, P_{2m-2} + (2m - 1) \, (P_{2m-1}) + \ldots \right.$$
$$\left. + 2P_2 + 1P_1 \right]$$

$$= \frac{1}{2m - 2} \sum_{d=1}^{2m-2} dP_d$$

$$= \frac{1}{2m-2} \sum_{d=0}^{2m-2} dP_d$$

$$= I$$

The penultimate step can be made since, whatever the value of P_0, the contribution to the summation of the term dP_d is zero for $d = 0$.

We have therefore shown that this geometric definition of intensity of fragmentation [equation (3.6)] is equivalent to the earlier definition [equation (3.5)]. The geometric derivation thus provides a rationale for the particular weighting scheme which we have used.

3.3 Examples

In this section, the use of I is illustrated by several examples. The first of these uses hypothetical opinion data, and the last two use some actual data on party preferences in the U.S. and Norway.

Dahl on the intensity of divisions

According to Professor Dahl, one reason "why the comparisons of intensities of preference is important arises from a desire to predict the stability of a democratic system and perhaps even to design rules to guarantee its stability" (Dahl 1956, p. 92). In his discussion of this problem, Dahl uses as an illustration the simple two-alternative case. The alternatives are "for" and "against" some policy, and it is assumed that in each of these groups, the citizens are subdivided into those strongly (R_3), moderately (R_2), or slightly (R_1) for or against. Dahl then groups the possible distributions into six different types (Dahl 1956, pp. 93–99). We have reproduced these in fig. 3.8, where the three intensity ranks are labeled 1, 2, 3. Although the six points are placed along the horizontal axis, this is not intended to imply that these six positions lie on some ordinal scale; and the dotted line between the two center points emphasizes that there are two nominal alternatives. This distinction be-

Figure 3.8

Six Hypothetical Distributions, with Two Alternatives
(For and Against) and Three Intensity Ranks
The frequencies are shown as percentages.
(From Robert A. Dahl, A Preface to Democratic Theory,
1956, chapter 4.)

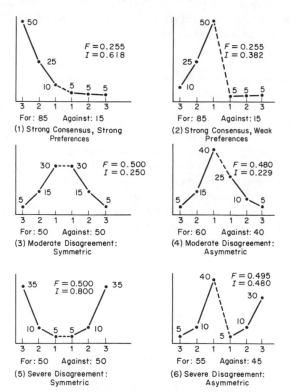

comes more important when there are more than two alternatives (and, of course, it would then be impossible to order all the intensity points in a diagram analogous to those used here).

Dahl suggests that the first four types are associated with regime stability, "that opinion on major issues in stable polyarchies tends to vary among these four types," but that a distribution of the fifth type poses a severe threat to the continued existence of the system. In the sixth type, disagreement is still severe (F is high), but only the less numerous side feels intensely. This is the case of an intense minority against an apathetic majority.

If we wished to relate opinion distributions to regime stability, we should have to ask how closely a distribution resembled one of these types. This could be done only by providing exact descriptions of such distributions. The two relevant descriptive parameters are the extent of fragmentation and the intensity of fragmentation (in the present example, the extent and intensity of disagreement). F alone is of course inadequate and must be qualified by I. For example, curves (3) and (5) of fig. 3.8 have the same value of F, but their implications for stability are likely to be enormously different (in fact, their I values are .25 and .80, respectively).

The values of F and I in our fig. 3.8 have been added to each of Dahl's six types.[25] We see that, in the first four cases, at least one of F and I is low (remembering that the maximum possible value of F is .5 when $n = 2$). But in the fifth case, both F and I are very high. Thus, if Dahl's conjecture is correct, stability is associated with distributions in which at least one of F and I is low. In the sixth case, F is fairly high (.495), while I is neither high nor low (.480). This, as we know, is the problematic distribution, the borderline case which may present special problems in a democratic system.

25. F and I were computed using the approximate forms for percentage data.

In an analysis of stability, then, we would consider stability not in terms of types, but as a function of the two variables F and I. The advantages of using F and I are even more striking when there are more than two alternatives ($n > 2$): for any number of alternatives (and any number of intensity ranks), we may summarize the data with only two variables. These two variables provide a complete description of "disagreement." In using them as explanatory variables in accounting for stability, for instance, we might conjecture that, for any values of n and m, stability is contingent upon at least one of F and I being sufficiently small. Furthermore, the use of F and I allows us to compare distributions based on different values of n (or m, or both). Without these parameters, such comparisons would be impossible.

Party identification in the United States[26]

Every other year, just before the congressional elections, the Survey Research Center of the University of Michigan conducts its well-known national survey. Since 1954, the following questions have been included:

Generally speaking, in politics, do you usually think of yourself as a Republican (R), a Democrat (D), an Independent, or what?

(If R or D) Would you call yourself a strong R or D or a not very strong R or D?

(If Independent or other) Do you think of yourself as closer to the R or D party?

There are two alternatives here: A_1—Democrats, and A_2—Republicans; and there are three intensity ranks: R_3—a strong R or D, R_2—a not very strong R or D, and R_1—an Independent, but closer to R or D. In 1964, the result of the sample was

26. The survey questions and data used in this section are taken from Survey Research Center (University of Michigan) codebooks.

	A$_1$	A$_2$
R$_1$	144	88
R$_2$	385	210
R$_3$	410	171
f$_i$	939	469

with N = 1408. From the bottom row of column sums (f$_i$), we compute F = .443, and the number of mixed pairs U = 443674. Since m = 3, the intensity distances (d) range from 0 to 4. The five P$_d$'s are found to be

P$_0$	P$_1$	P$_2$	P$_3$	P$_4$
.0286	.1445	.3204	.3458	.1607

(which sum to unity, as they should); and from the formula given above by equation (3.5), we find that I = .616.

We note, parenthetically, the remarkable stability of the values of F and I between 1954 and 1964. Using Survey Research Center data for these years, in the same way as in the example just given, we find the following values for F and I.

	1954	1956	1958	1960	1962	1964
F	.467	.490	.467	.485	.478	.443
I	.612	.616	.634	.630	.618	.616

It should be remembered that when n = 2, the maximum possible value of F is .5 (and would occur if the sample was equally divided between Democrats and Republicans), but that for any value of F, I may take any value from 0 (when all the sample is at R$_1$) to 1 (when all the sample is at R$_3$).

Party identification in Norway

Our final example uses survey data on party identification in Norway, which are similar to those used in the previous example, but with n = 5 and m = 2. The two intensity ranks correspond to "strong identification" (R_2) and "weak identification" (R_1). The data and the five alternatives (political parties) are as follows:[27]

	Labor	Liberal	Christian People's	Agrarian	Conservative
	A_1	A_2	A_3	A_4	A_5
(Weak) R_1	144	75	23	50	47
(Strong) R_2	123	27	36	34	28
f_i	267	102	59	84	75

For these data, it is found that F = .717 and I = .417, and we see that when F is large, I need not be.

3.4 Summary

Starting from the partition, introduced in chapter 2, of the set of all pairs of individuals into matched pairs and mixed pairs, we have further partitioned the latter by considering the proportion of mixed pairs whose members are separated by a distance d for each possible value of d. These proportions— P_0, P_1, . . . , P_{2m-2} —were then expressed directly in terms of the frequencies f_{ij}. I, the intensity of fragmentation, was defined as a sum of

27. The data are taken from table 13.2 of Campbell and Valen (chapter 13 in Campbell, Converse, Miller, and Stokes 1966). The survey was conducted in 1957 in the province of Rogaland, but Campbell and Valen believe that the corresponding data for the whole of Norway would not be substantially different. The questions used to elicit this data are to be found in this article.

weighted P_d's, with each P_d being weighted by its corresponding intensity distance d.

The two measures, F and I, give a description of fragmentation over any single cleavage. F measures the "extent" to which a system is fragmented into nominal groups, with no account taken of variations in the intensity with which individuals cleave to their various groups. It characterizes both the number of groups and the distribution of individuals over these groups. F, however, may have the same value for a distribution in which all individuals cleave to their positions (groups) very intensely and a distribution in which all positions are held almost indifferently. With opinion cleavages, for example, the former distribution, if F is high, would correspond to considerable dissensus (and possible conflict), while the latter would correspond to greater consensus (and conflict would be less likely). Clearly, F must be qualified. This further detail is provided by the measure I, which we have called the intensity of fragmentation.

CHAPTER 4: CROSS-CUTTING CLEAVAGES

4.1 Introduction

So far, we have considered only single cleavages; and in many problems it is indeed sufficient to analyze the fragmentation (heterogeneity, dissensus, or fractionalization) produced by each cleavage separately. Two types of explanation of democratic stability, for example, fall into this category. First there are the "consensus theories," which seek to account for the viability of democracies either in terms of an underlying consensus in the society on fundamental democratic principles[1] or in terms of patterns of "differentiated agreement" — in which it is argued that, in stable democracies, there is more consensus among the politically active than among the electorate generally.[2] Second, there are various "social pluralism" arguments. Here some writers have argued that too much heterogeneity over social (mainly racial, linguistic, and religious) cleavages is detrimental to stable democracy; others that too much homogeneity is likewise detrimental. Later, we shall return to discuss social pluralism. For the moment, we note that both the consensus theories and the social pluralism theories, although concerned with the effects of several cleavages, are not focused upon the relations between these cleavages but rather upon the fragmentation produced by each cleavage separately.

1. For example, Barker 1958. See the discussion of Griffith, Plamenatz, and Pennock 1956, pp. 101–37; and the criticisms by Prothro and Grigg 1960, pp. 270–94, and McCloskey 1964, pp. 361–82.
2. See Dahl 1961, chapter 28; McCloskey 1964; and Budge 1970, which is devoted entirely to testing this theory.

But the third main type of explanation of democratic stability is concerned with these effects of relations between cleavages — the extent to which cleavages cross-cut or reinforce one another. Cross-cutting cleavages are the subject of the present chapter.

The importance of the concept of cross-cutting is well established in political science: (1) in the study of individual voting behavior and the birth and growth of political parties, (2) in the study of conflict and its resolution, and (3) in the study of democratic stability. Of course, these three broad areas are not independent; but they have provided different foci in the study of cross-cutting cleavages.

The first is concerned with a variety of "cross-pressures" hypotheses. Very briefly, the arguments are as follows. If an individual is a member of several groups (primary groups, such as family and friendship groups; secondary groups, especially associations; or categoric groups, such as social class, race, religion, and region) with different political norms pulling him in different political directions, he is said to be "cross-pressured." As a result, he might lose interest in the campaign, be late in deciding which party to vote for, make changes in his voting intention, feel a reduced sense of partisanship, repress one or more of the cross-pressuring stimuli, abstain from voting, or split his vote between competing parties.[3] Clearly, there are a multitude of propositions here; but they are all concerned with the effects on an individual, at the preelection stage and at voting time, of his membership in groups having different political opinions.

In addition to studies of the social bases of voting behavior, which have been concerned with the cross-cutting

3. The first studies of voting using the idea of cross-pressures were Tingsten 1937; and, more explicitly, Lazarsfeld, Berelson, and Gaudet 1944. It has appeared in the subsequent U.S. voting studies. See the discussions in Lane 1959, pp. 197–203; and Lipset 1959, chapter 6.

of party affiliation and various social cleavages such as class and religion,[4] there is growing interest in the historical development of voter alignments and party systems. This is concerned not only with the cross-cutting of party and social cleavages, but also with the relation between party competition on the one hand and the cross-cutting of politically relevant social cleavages on the other.[5]

In the work of the sociologists Simmel (1955) and Ross (1920), cross-cutting cleavages are seen as regulators of the growth of major conflict in a society. In his study, The Functions of Social Conflict, based on Simmel's work, Lewis Coser (1956, pp. 72–81) writes:

> The interdependence of antagonistic groups and the crisscrossing within such societies of conflicts, which serve to "sew the social system together" by cancelling each other out, thus prevent disintegration along one primary line of cleavage.

This reduction of conflict could occur in two related ways. One is through the modification of individual attitudes and behaviors — not only through cross-pressures at election time, as described above, but by reducing the intensity of individual political feelings in general. In Lipset's words, "Multiple and potentially inconsistent affiliations, loyalties, and stimuli reduce the emotion and aggressiveness involved in political choice" (Lipset 1960, p. 88). Secondly, the more cross-cutting there is, the smaller the number of persons who are in the same group in both cleavages, and hence the more difficult it is to build a coalition or potential conflict group containing only individuals who have no links with the opposition, i.e., who agree on all their

4. See, for example, Alford 1963.

5. See, for example, Lipset and Rokkan 1967, and Allardt and Littunen 1964.

memberships. [6] Dahrendorf was probably thinking of both ways of reducing conflict when he said that it "seems plausible that there is a close positive correlation between the degree of superimposition of conflicts and their intensity." [7]

These arguments concerning the reduction of conflict through cross-cutting have also been used by several writers whose main focus has been on the conditions necessary to democratic stability. Seymour Martin Lipset argues that

> a stable democracy requires a situation in which all the major political parties include supporters from many segments of the population. A system in which the support of different parties corresponds too closely to basic social divisions cannot continue on a democratic basis, for it reflects a state of conflict so intense and clear-cut as to rule out compromise. [Lipset 1960, p. 31]

And he maintains that

> the available evidence suggests that the changes for stable democracy are enhanced to the extent that groups and individuals have a number of cross-cutting, politically relevant affiliations. [Lipset 1960, pp. 88–89]

In the work of David Truman, the emphasis is on the compromise which must take place within each group (whose members may also belong to other groups) in order for the group to survive, since "the cohesion and in-

---

6. Robert Dahl has mentioned this in connection with the formation of "majority" coalitions: "If most individuals in the society identify themselves with more than one group, then there is some positive probability that any majority contains individuals who identify themselves for certain purposes with the threatened minority" (Dahl 1956, pp. 104–05).

7. Dahrendorf 1959, p. 215. See also the discussion of "the intensity of fragmentation and the intensity of conflict" in section 4.5 below.

fluence of the affected group depend upon the incorpora-
tion or accommodation of the conflicting loyalties of any
significant segment of the group, an accommodation that
may result in altering the original claims."[8] Despite this
emphasis on the internal stability of groups, Truman's
approach is basically similar to Lipset's: the stability of
the entire system depends upon tolerance and compromise
between groups, but this is possible only if adjustments
are made within each group (or merely by its leaders) so
that the claims of one group upon another are tempered
in accordance with the diverse interests of its members.
For example, "the leaders of a Parent-Teacher Association must take some account of the fact that their proposals must be acceptable to members who also belong to
the local taxpayers' league, to the local Chamber of Commerce, and to the Catholic Church" (Truman 1951, p. 509).

These explanations of democratic stability in terms
of cross-cutting cleavages have, of course, been criti-
cized.[9] But the truth or falsehood of the arguments does
not directly concern us here; even if the critics are correct, the criticisms themselves raise questions which cannot be answered without a clear understanding of cross-
cutting.

In this brief introduction, we have attempted to indicate the very central place of cross-cutting cleavages in
much of political science. We now turn to an explication
of the cross-cutting concept. After defining it, we shall
consider the relations between the amount of cross-cutting
of two cleavages and the amounts of fragmentation (F)
produced by each cleavage separately. Then we shall
briefly explore some implications of these relations for
the theories of democratic stability based on social pluralism and cross-cutting cleavages. Our discussion, focused
not on theory construction per se but on the formation of
a concept through definition, will, we hope, provide some

8. Truman 1951, p. 509. Truman's approach derives from
Bentley 1908.

9. See, for example, Mitchell 1963.

90

support for Hempel's belief that "concept formation and theory formation in science are so closely related as to constitute virtually two different aspects of the same procedure" (Hempel 1952, pp. 1–2).

4.2 The Definition of "Cross-Cutting"

For simplicity, we shall consider only two cleavages at a time, although our measure could be extended in several ways to deal with more than two. We call these two cleavages X_1 and X_2.

Before proceeding to a definition of cross-cutting, let us be clear about the universe of individuals under consideration. Earlier we defined "crystallization" (C) for a given cleavage as the proportion of the community having a definite position; we noted that C usually equals 1.0 for trait cleavages, but not for opinion or behavioral cleavages. Thus, corresponding to the two cleavages X_1 and X_2, there are two (possibly different) crystallized portions of the community. C_1 and C_2 will be used to denote the crystallization (the value of C) for X_1 and X_2 respectively. At one extreme, the crystallized portions are identical, that is, they consist of the same individuals; at the other extreme, they are entirely distinct. Clearly, the "cross-cutting" of two cleavages can be defined only with respect to that part of the community which is crystallized on both cleavages. This is pictured in fig. 4.1.

We define the "overlap" between two cleavages as the proportion of the number of people crystallized by either cleavage who are crystallized on both cleavages.[10] Thus

$$\text{overlap} = \frac{\text{number crystallized on } X_1 \text{ and } X_2}{\text{number crystallized on } X_1 \text{ or } X_2} = C'$$

10. It is unfortunate that there is some terminological confusion in the literature here: "cross-cutting" is invariably used in the way it is used here, but the term "overlapping" has been used to mean cross-cutting and also its opposite, reinforcing! "Overlap" seems entirely suited to the present meaning.

Figure 4.1

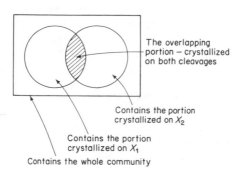

The overlapping
portion — crystallized
on both cleavages

Contains the portion
crystallized on X_2

Contains the portion
crystallized on X_1

Contains the whole community

For attitudinal cleavages, C' may be quite small: the individuals who have an opinion on one issue may be quite distinct, or almost distinct, from those having an opinion on another issue, and we call this situation one of distinct "issue-publics." For trait cleavages, on the other hand, C' will usually be fairly high. If the two cleavages are social class and religion, for example, then crystallization will presumably be almost 1.0 on the first cleavage, and so C' will have roughly the same value as crystallization on the second cleavage. This will vary considerably, depending upon the proportion who are areligious.

Henceforth, when we speak of the cross-cutting of two cleavages, we shall be referring only to cross-cutting within the overlapping portion. For this reason, a value obtained from our index of cross-cutting may be misleading when considered alone, and it should always be evaluated together with the value of C'.

We may now define our terms. Suppose that the two cleavages, X_1 and X_2, are of the type considered in chapter 2 — that each cleavage divides the corresponding crystallized portion of the community into nominal groups. Let X_1 and X_2 contain n and n_2 groups respectively (n_1 need not equal n_2). We might, for example, define three social classes ($n_1 = 3$) and two religions ($n_2 = 2$). Let F_1 and F_2 be the fragmentation, as defined in chapter 2, produced by X_1 and X_2 respectively. F_1 and F_2 are calculated separately for each cleavage, but in each case the value is based upon only those individuals in the overlapping portion. We continue to use the terms "matched" and "mixed pairs": a pair of individuals is "matched on X_1" if the two are in the same nominal group with respect to the cleavage X_1 and "mixed on X_1" if they are in different groups. The same applies to X_2.

If, in the above example, all those who held a particular religion were also in the same class (and vice versa) so that the two sets of groups (corresponding to X_1 and X_2) were identical, then the two cleavages are said to "reinforce" each other. If, however, some of those who were of a particular religion were divided among several social classes, then we say that the two cleavages "cross-cut" each other. Cross-cutting, then, is the extent to which individuals who are in the same group on one cleavage are in different groups on the other cleavage.

Thus, we shall define "cross-cutting" (XC) to be the proportion of all pairs of individuals whose two members are in the same group of one cleavage but in different groups of the other cleavage. Let A be the number of pairs whose members are in the same group of X_1 but in different groups of X_2 (i.e., matched on X_1 but mixed on X_2), and let B be the number of pairs whose members are in different groups of X_1 but in the same group of X_2 (i.e., mixed on X_1 but matched on X_2). Then, since the total number of pairs is $N'(N'-1)/2$, where N' is the number of individuals in the overlap, our measure of cross-cutting is

$$XC = \frac{A+B}{N'(N'-1)/2} \tag{4.1}$$

Before examining the properties of XC and giving an example of its use, we first express it in a form which is more convenient for computational purposes. In the usual way for cross-classifications, we define a contingency table. Denote the element in the ith row and the jth column of this table by x_{ij}. Let the ith row sum (marginal frequency) be $x_{i.}$ — this is the number of individuals in the ith group of the cleavage X_1. Denote the jth column sum (marginal frequency) by $x_{.j}$ — this is the number of individuals in the jth group of X_2. The corresponding proportions will be denoted by p_{ij}, $p_{i.}$, and $p_{.j}$ ($p_{ij} = x_{ij}/N'$, etc.). Table 4.1 below is an example of such a contingency table; both raw frequencies and proportions (in parentheses) are shown, and the marginal totals are also given.[11] An expression for XC in terms of the elements x_{ij} of the contingency table will now be derived. It is far from obvious that the end result, given by equation (4.2) below, is equivalent to the initial expression in equation (4.1), but if the reader wishes to take it on faith, he may pass over the following mathematics.

The number of pairs of individuals which are in the same group of X_1 but in different groups of X_2 is

$$A = \sum_{i=1}^{n_1} \sum_{\substack{j=1 \\ \text{all } k > j}}^{n_2-1} x_{ij} x_{ik}$$

$$= \frac{1}{2} \sum_{i=1}^{n_1} \sum_{j=1}^{n_2} x_{ij}(x_{i.} - x_{ij})$$

The number of pairs of individuals which are in different groups of X_1 but in the same group of X_2 is

$$B = \sum_{k=1}^{n_2} \sum_{\substack{i=1 \\ \text{all } j > i}}^{n_1-1} x_i \ x_j$$

$$= \frac{1}{2} \sum_{i=1}^{n_1} \sum_{j=1}^{n_2} x_{ij}(x_{.j} - x_{ij})$$

11. Table 4.1 is adapted from table 5 of Allardt and Pesonen (chapter 7 of Lipset and Rokkan 1967), p. 342. The original source is the Finnish Gallup Poll of 1958. Social class was defined by occupation, but almost identical results were obtained when self-identification was used as the criterion. The proportions are based on those who do have a preference for some party.

Table 4.1

A Cross-Classification of Party Preference
by Social Class

Social Class (X_2)

		Farmer	Worker	White Collar	Marginal Totals
Party Preference (X_1)	Social Democrats	9 (.013)	143 (.198)	19 (.026)	171 (.237)
	Communists	28 (.039)	143 (.198)	7 (.010)	171 (.247)
	Agrarians	166 (.230)	21 (.029)	7 (.010)	194 (.269)
	Bourgeois (3 parties)	52 (.072)	46 (.064)	81 (.112)	179 (.248)
	Marginal Totals	255 (.353)	353 (.489)	114 (.158)	722 (1.0)
	No party preference	52	67	20	139

Thus

$$XC = \frac{A+B}{N'(N'-1)/2}$$

$$= \frac{1/2}{N'(N'-1)/2} \left[\sum_i \sum_j x_{ij} x_{i.} + \sum_i \sum_j x_{ij} x_{.j} - 2\sum_i \sum_j x^2_{ij} \right]$$

$$= \frac{1}{N'(N'-1)} \left[\sum_i (x_{i.} \sum_j x_{ij}) + \sum_j (x_{.j} \sum_i x_{ij}) - 2\sum_{i,j} x^2_{ij} \right]$$

$$= \frac{1}{N'(N'-1)} \left[\sum_i x^2_{i.} + \sum_j x^2_{.j} - 2\sum_{i,j} x^2_{ij} \right] \qquad (4.2)$$

If N' is large enough for the approximation $1/N'(N'-1) = 1/(N')^2$ to hold, then this may be written

$$XC = \sum_i p^2_{i.} + \sum_j p^2_{.j} - 2\sum_{i,j} p^2_{ij} \qquad (4.3)$$

The final summation is over all the cells of the table.

This expression for XC is now very simple for computational purposes. Before commenting on it, its use will be illustrated, using the data given in table 4.1. These data are from a Finnish national survey of 1958. The two cleavages are party preference (X_1) with $n_1 = 4$, and social class (X_2) with $n_2 = 3$. There is maximum crystallization $(C_2 = 1)$ on X_2, since every individual is assigned to a social class. But, as indicated in the lower part of the table, a total of 139 respondents have no party preference. Thus N' = 722 and N = 722 + 139 = 861. Hence the crystallization on X_1 is $C_1 = 722/861 = .839$, so the overlap (C') is also .839. Since N' is large enough for the approximation mentioned above to hold, we use equation (4.3) to compute the value of XC. From the proportions given in parentheses in table 4.1, we calculate

$$\sum_i p^2_{i.} = (.237)^2 + (.247)^2 + (.269)^2 + (.248)^2$$
$$= .251$$

Similarly

$$\sum_j p^2_{.j} = (.353)^2 + (.489)^2 + (.158)^2$$
$$= .389$$

and

$$\sum_{i,j} p^2_{ij} = (.013)^2 + (.198)^2 + (.026)^2$$
$$+ (.039)^2 + \ldots$$
$$= .156$$

Inserting these values in equation (4.3), we find that XC = .251 + .389 - 2(.156), i.e., XC = .327.

Returning now to the expression for XC given in equation (4.3) above, we notice that

$$\sum_i p^2_{i\cdot}$$

is the probability that two individuals, drawn at random from the total set of N', belong to the same nominal group of X_1.[12] In other words, we have

$$1 - \sum_{i=1}^{n_1} p^2_{i\cdot} = F_1$$

where F_1 is the fragmentation of cleavage X_1. Similarly

$$1 - \sum_{j=1}^{n_2} p^2_{\cdot j} = F_2$$

where F_2 is the fragmentation of cleavage X_2. We also define

$$F_c = 1 - \sum_{i=1}^{n_1} \sum_{j=1}^{n_2} p^2_{ij}$$

which is the probability that any two individuals are in different "cells" of the contingency table, i.e., that they are in different groups in at least one of the cleavages.

The expression for XC in equation (4.3) can now be written

$$XC = (1 - F_1) + (1 - F_2) - 2(1 - F_c)$$

i.e.

$$XC = 2F_c - F_1 - F_2 \qquad (4.4)$$

12. This, of course, also depends on the approximation introduced above. Assuming that the two individuals are drawn at random, without replacement of the first, then, strictly speaking, this probability is:

$$\sum_i \frac{x_{i\cdot}(x_{i\cdot} - 1)}{N'(N' - 1)}$$

This striking result shows how cross-cutting and the fragmentation of the two cleavages are related. It will be useful in examining the properties of XC and in our discussion of theories of democratic stability (section 4.5).

4.3 Some Properties of the Measure

1. The measure XC varies between limits of 0 and 1.
2. The smallest possible value of XC is zero. This occurs when all the matched pairs on X_1 are matched on X_2 and all the mixed pairs on X_1 are mixed on X_2, in which case cleavages are said to be "completely reinforcing." This occurs when and only when the groups are identical for both cleavages—thus $n_1 = n_2$ and $F_1 = F_2 = F_c$.
3. The hypothetical case of complete cross-cutting would occur, by definition, if all matched pairs on X_1 were mixed on X_2 and all mixed pairs on X_1 were matched on X_2. The corresponding value of XC would then be 1. But this could only occur if the cleavage X_1 consisted of only one group, while each group of the other cleavage X_2 contained only one individual. X_1 is not a cleavage, as we have defined it; hence this case is inadmissible, and complete cross-cutting cannot occur.

This result can be demonstrated quite simply. Consider the very simple cleavage (X_1, say) shown in fig. 4.2, where individuals in the same group have been joined by a solid line and those in different groups have been joined by a broken line.

Figure 4.2

A Cleavage Consisting of Two Groups

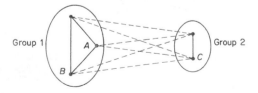

Can we construct a second cleavage (X_2) which will completely cross-cut X_1? Consider the triangle of individuals ABC. If X_2 completely cross-cuts X_1, then A and B must be in different groups of X_2, A and C must be in the same group, and B and C must be in the same group, so that the triangle ABC in X_1 would become

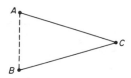

in X_2. This is clearly absurd, since, if A and B are each in the same group as C, then they must be in the same group as one another. This proof will hold for any values of $n_1(\geq 2)$ and $n_2(\geq 2)$, since one of the cleavages will always contain at least one triangle like ABC — with two broken lines and one solid line.

We have shown that the assumption of complete cross-cutting leads to an absurdity — XC can never equal 1. But suppose now that X_1 divides the community into two groups, one containing 95 individuals and the other containing 5 (this is now a cleavage), while each group of X_2 contains only one individual. Then, while most of the pairs are matched in X_1, they all become mixed in X_2 (since X_2 has no matched pairs at all); and there are only a few mixed pairs in X_1, which are still mixed in X_2. Thus XC will be nearly 1.0.

Only in cases like this, where there is very low fragmentation on one cleavage and very high fragmentation on the other, can there be much cross-cutting. Such cases are empirically unlikely, but our measure must be general; i.e., it must be defined so as to yield a value for all possible pairs of cleavages. Thus, 1.0 can almost be attained and must be taken as the upper bound of XC. In fact, it can be shown that the maximum value of XC is

$$\frac{N'}{N'-1} \max \left\{ 1 - \frac{1}{n_1}, \; 1 - \frac{1}{n_2} \right\}$$

4. Given F_1 and F_2, what are the upper and lower bounds on the possible values of XC? It is of considerable interest, as we shall see later, to know the relation between XC on the one hand and F_1 and F_2 on the other. Given two cleavages (i.e., given the two fragmentation values F_1 and F_2, but not the arrangement of individuals within the various groups), how much and how little cross-cutting can there be? F_1 and F_2 do not completely determine XC, since, as can be seen from the relation XC = $2F_c - F_1 - F_2$ obtained above, F_c can take on several values for given fixed values of F_1 and F_2. But F_1 and F_2 do constrain the possible values of XC. The object here is not to be able to infer the approximate value of XC from a knowledge of F_1 and F_2, but to see what constraints F_1 and F_2 place upon the possibilities for cross-cutting.

We denote by max XC and min XC the largest and smallest possible values of XC, given F_1 and F_2. There is no simple relation between F_1, F_2 and max XC, or between F_1, F_2 and min XC, but we shall be able to make some interesting inferences about these relations.

If F_1 and F_2 are both very low (i.e., the cleavages are not very fragmented), then F_c must also be low. The reader may convince himself of this by experimenting with a few contingency tables. Hence, from the relation XC = $2F_c - F_1 - F_2$, we see that XC must be low. An example is shown in fig. 4.3, in which the numbered shapes enclose individuals belonging to the same group. No individuals are named, so that no indication is given in the diagram of the amount of cross-cutting.

Clearly, most of the pairs of X_1 must be matched, since most of the individuals are in group 1. Further, most of those in group 1 of X_1 must be in group 1 of X_2. Thus, even if those in groups 2 and 3 of X_2 were in group 1 of X_2, most matched pairs of X_1 are matched on X_2 also. From the definition of XC given in equation (4.1), it is clear that the maximum possible cross-cutting here is very low. As F_1 and F_2 approach zero (i.e., as more and more of the individuals are in just one group, in each cleavage), max XC also approaches zero.

Suppose now that F_1 and F_2 are both very high. Then most of the pairs of X_1 are mixed, and they must be mixed on X_2 also. Very little cross-cutting is possible; max XC and min XC are small and approach 0 as F_1 and F_2 approach 1. This can also be inferred directly from the relation $XC = 2F_c - F_1 - F_2$. If F_1 and F_2 are high, so that F_c is also high, then XC must be low.

These last two results, taken together, mean that there cannot be much cross-cutting whenever F_1 and F_2 are both very low or both very high. The implications of this will be taken up later.

Now suppose that F_1 is low and F_2 is high.[13] Figure 4.4 shows an example. Here, most of the pairs of X_1 are matched, and most of them must be mixed on X_2. Thus, max XC is high. Furthermore, a small amount of cross-cutting is also impossible; min XC is also high. As F_1 approaches 0 and F_2 approaches 1, both max XC and min XC approach 1. Again, this can be inferred from the relation $XC = 2F_c - F_1 - F_2$.

As F_2 increases, with F_1 remaining small, it is clear that max XC and min XC increase. Consider, as an intermediate example, the two cleavages shown in fig. 4.5. In X_1, 8/9 of the individuals are in one group and 1/9 in a second group. X_2 consists of two equal groups. Assuming N' to be large, the fragmentation on the first cleavage is

$$F_1 = 1 - [(8/9)^2 + (1/9)^2] = 16/81$$

which is fairly low. For X_2, we find $F_2 = 1/2$. Maximum cross-cutting would occur if the individuals corresponded across cleavages in the way indicated by the shading in

13. The labeling of the two cleavages, X_1 and X_2, is of course arbitrary. These results are all symmetrical; in this case, for example, it does not matter which of the two cleavages has high and which has low fragmentation.

101

Figure 4.3

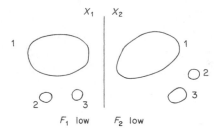

F_1 low F_2 low

Figure 4.4

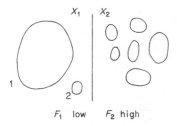

F_1 low F_2 high

Figure 4.5

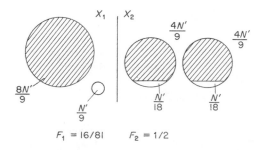

$F_1 = 16/81$ $F_2 = 1/2$

fig. 4.5: each of the two groups of X_1 is divided equally between the two groups of X_2.[14] We then have

$$A = \left(\frac{4N'}{9}\right)^2 + \left(\frac{N'}{18}\right)^2$$

$$B = 2\left(\frac{4N'}{9}\right)\left(\frac{N'}{18}\right)$$

Hence, after some manipulation, we find that

$$\max XC = \frac{A+B}{N'(N'-1)/2} = \frac{1}{2} \cdot \frac{(N')^2}{N'(N'-1)}$$

and since N' is large, $\max XC = 1/2$, approximately.

As two final examples, we note that if $F_1 = F_2 = 1/2$, then it can be shown that $\max XC$ is also $1/2$ (if N' is large), and if $F_1 = F_2 = 1/3$, then $\max XC$ is approximately $4/9$. In both cases, since $F_1 = F_2$, the minimum possible value of XC is zero.

In addition to the pictorial examples given above, the reader might experiment with a few hypothetical contingency tables, calculating F_1, F_2 and F_c, and then using the relation $XC = 2F_c - F_1 - F_2$ to obtain XC. In this way he will obtain a fuller picture of the relation between F_1 and F_2 on the one hand, and XC on the other.

If F_1 and F_2 are approximately equal, then, as they both vary between 0 and 1, the curve of $\max XC$ is roughly as shown in fig. 4.6. Clearly, cross-cutting can be as low as zero for any value of $F_1 (= F_2)$, so the curve of $\min XC$ is simply the horizontal line at the base of fig. 4.6. This figure will be of interest later, when we discuss the possible relationship between cross-cutting and social pluralism. For the moment we note that, although the exact shape of the curve is uncertain, it is clear (as we saw earlier) that when F_1 and F_2 are both low (near 0) or both

14. That this gives maximum cross-cutting seems reasonable, but it is not obvious. We return to this point in the next section.

high (near 1), there cannot be much cross-cutting (XC must be low). In fact, high values of XC can only occur when one of the cleavages has low fragmentation and the other has high fragmentation.

Figure 4.6

Curve of max XC Plotted Against F_1 (= F_2)

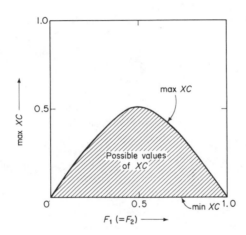

4.4 Cross-Cutting and Measures of Association

Most discussions of cross-cutting cleavages in the literature of political science are based directly upon the contingency table, and no attempt is made to indicate precisely the amount of cross-cutting. Occasionally, even when the investigation is concerned with cross-cutting and its consequences, a χ^2-test is made for "statistical association" between the two cleavages (nominal variables), and perhaps a measure of the strength of the association is also used. We will show in this section that cross-cutting and statistical association are two different things, and that the use of a measure of association in place of a measure of cross-cutting could be misleading. [15]

First of all, we note that χ^2 simply measures the deviation from statistical independence, where "statistical independence" here means that $p_{ij} = p_{i.} \, p_{.j}$ for all i and j. Several measures based on χ^2 have been proposed as measures of association— the mean square contingency (ϕ^2), the coefficient of contingency (C), Tschuprow's T, and Cramer's V. [16] None of these statistics (and the first two are widely used in the social sciences) [17] can be given an operational interpretation (cf. Blalock 1960, and Goodman and Kruskal 1954, pp. 732–64); nor is it meaningful to compare their values for two tables of different sizes, i.e., different values of n_1 or n_2 or both (cf. Blalock 1960; Goodman and Kruskal 1954; and Siegel 1956, p. 201). This last property, which would prohibit their use especially in empirical work in comparative politics, is alone sufficient to rule out such statistics as measures of cross-cutting. Furthermore, all these χ^2-like statistics have a value of zero when the cleavages are statistically independent (remembering that association and cross-cutting run, as it were, in opposite directions, so that if we were to base a measure of cross-cutting on C, for example, then we should use 1–C). Consider the following simple examples (where the marginal frequencies are also shown), each of which is a case of statistical independence.

15. The remarks in this section do not imply criticisms of any of the measures of association qua measures of association. For some problems, such measures would be required. But where one is dealing explicitly with the concept of cross-cutting, as in studying the relation between cross-cutting and democratic stability, then a measure of cross-cutting, rather than a measure of association, is clearly required.

16. These statistics are defined in Blalock 1960, pp. 228–30.

17. A rare use of Cramer's V is mentioned by Alford (chapter 1 in Lipset and Rokkan 1967).

.25	.25	.5
.25	.25	.5
.5	.5	1.0

(1)

.24	.24	.24	.24	.96
.01	.01	.01	.01	.04
.25	.25	.25	.25	1.0

(2)

In (1) we have $F_1 = F_2 = .5$ and $F_c = .75$, so that $XC = .5$. In (2) we have $F_1 = .0768$, $F_2 = .75$, $F_c = .769$, so that $XC = .711$. But in both cases the measures of association mentioned above have the value of zero!

Several measures of association devised by Goodman and Kruskal do have operational interpretations, unlike χ^2-like statistics, but they too have a value of zero in the case of statistical independence. [18]

Statistical association is really cross-cutting, but with the marginal frequencies normed out. That is, measures of association, since they are measures of the extent to which group membership on one cleavage can be predicted from group membership on the other, are constructed to be independent of the marginal frequencies (and hence, of F_1 and F_2). Thus, as much association is possible between two highly fragmented cleavages as between two less fragmented cleavages; whereas there cannot be very much cross-cutting, as we have defined it, between two highly fragmented cleavages. There is so much disagreement in such cleavages that it is just not possible for it to be completely reduced through cross-cutting.

4.5 Cross-Cutting Cleavages, Social Pluralism, and Theories of Democratic Stability

At the start of this chapter, three approaches to the explanation of democratic stability were mentioned. These are based on the notions of (1) consensus, (2) social pluralism, and (3) cross-cutting cleavages. Most theories of

18. See Goodman and Kruskal 1954, and 1959, pp. 123–63. Their tau statistic is closest to XC in appearance.

democratic stability belong to one of these three types.[19]
Crucial to all of them is the concept of political cleavage,
in one of its forms.[20]

The first approach is concerned mainly with opinion
cleavages and the consensus−dissensus continuum.[21] The
second involves trait cleavages— such as race, religion,
language, and region— and the homogeneity−heterogeneity
continuum. It includes several different arguments, which
will be summarized below.   The third approach also includes a variety of explanations, which were described
earlier, but the main theme is clear.

> Proposition 1: If there is not sufficient cross-cutting
> between politically relevant cleavages, then demo-
> cratic political organization is not likely to be
> stable.[22]

In all three approaches, the various conditions for stable
democracy are statements about the concepts which have
been the subject of this monograph.

When the cleavage terms of the social pluralism and
cross-cutting theories are defined in the ways we have
suggested, then these two approaches are seen to be highly
related.   This relation is the subject of the remainder of

19. Cf. Budge 1970, chapter 1. Budge's review of theories
of democratic stability does not include the social pluralism
group, although groups (1) and (2) are, of course, related.

20. See the introduction to chapter 1, above, where three
types of cleavages (traits, opinions, behaviors) were introduced.

21. The measures of consensus which have been used in
some of these studies are discussed in appendix A.   Measures
of consensus based on stronger assumptions about the alternatives (groups) can be found in appendix B.

22. The logical status of this and the subsequent statements
labeled "propositions" is not our concern here.   Neither
are we providing an analysis of the corresponding "theories,"
which are, in each case, arguments connecting the two parts of
the propositions stated here.

this section, and should serve as an illustration not only of some possible uses of our measures, but also of the way in which concept formation and theory formation are interwoven. First, however, a brief summary of the social pluralist arguments must be given.

The social pluralist arguments

In his very interesting analysis of Dutch politics, Arendt Lijphart (1968, chapter 1) articulates the widespread assumption that, "viable democratic government faces grave obstacles in so-called 'plural societies,' that is, societies with clearly discernible racial, linguistic, and religious differences." This common presupposition, first argued by Aristotle, corresponds to the following proposition.

Proposition 2: If a society is too heterogeneous over racial, linguistic, and religious cleavages, then democratic political organization is not likely to be stable.

But, as Lijphart also points out, a number of eminent theorists, beginning perhaps with John Stuart Mill, have argued an apparently opposite position, which might be put this way.

Proposition 3: If a society is too homogeneous over racial, linguistic, and religious cleavages, then democratic political organization is not likely to be stable.

Lijphart quite rightly draws his reader's attention to the fact that these two propositions need not be considered contradictory: "The difference is merely one of degree. A democracy . . . must have both a minimum of social homogeneity and a minimum of heterogeneity" (Lijphart 1968, p. 4). By conceiving homogeneity and heterogeneity in degrees, we may state another proposition, which subsumes both of the initial statements. Consider this diagram:

108

Figure 4.7

Proposition 2 suggests that all democracy-supporting societies lie to the left of point A, and proposition 3 suggests that these same societies must lie to the right of B. These points may be interpreted as values of F.

Only if we assume that there is no space which is to the left of A and also to the right of B do these two propositions contradict each other. Assuming that some such space exists, it is not absurd to formulate another proposition.

Proposition 4: If a society is either too homogeneous or too heterogeneous over racial, linguistic, and religious cleavages, then democratic political organization is not likely to be stable.

This proposition suggests that all democracy-supporting societies lie on the segment AB as we have drawn it, and it is a more interesting suggestion than either of the predecessors. We have, then, two hypothetical thresholds for social heterogeneity (A and B), and we suggest that only societies which are above the one (B) and yet below the other (A) can sustain democratic political organization.

Assuming that the politically relevant cleavages, or at least those cleavages which divide the community into potential conflict groups, can be identified, several questions arise. "With how many and how deep differences can a democracy exist before approaching the danger zone of dissension, revolt, and dissolution?" (Lijphart 1968, p. 4). How does democratic stability depend on the relation between cleavages? If the community is divided by only one relevant cleavage (X_1, say), then perhaps the social pluralism theory would be concerned simply with the relation between stability and the fragmentation produced by that cleavage. But suppose there are two relevant cleavages, X_1 and X_2. Does proposition 4 have to be true for each cleavage? Are the thresholds for social heterogeneity the same for each cleavage? What are the "joint" effects of the two cleavages? For instance, how does stability vary as a function of both F_1 and F_2? As soon as we begin to attempt to answer these questions, we are forced to think about the relations between cleavages, i.e., about cross-cutting. It is not, then, surprising that our measures of cross-cutting and fragmentation should be formally related. Let us examine this more closely, and see how these measures forge links between the two theories of democratic stability.[23]

Social pluralism and cross-cutting cleavages

We assume that F (fragmentation) is used as the measure of heterogeneity in the social pluralism arguments; and we simplify the problem by restricting our attention to two cleavages, X_1 and X_2. Let the values of F associated with X_1 and X_2 be F_1 and F_2 respectively.[24] Then proposition 4 might be reformulated as

23. Although the consensus theories are also based on cleavage concepts, they are not formally related to the social pluralism and cross-cutting theories in the way that these two are related to each other. The consensus theories are concerned with opinion cleavages; the other two with trait and behavioral cleavages. Empirically, however, one would expect all three types of cleavage to be related, and a completely unified theory of democratic stability may have to take all these relations into account.

24. In the social pluralism theories, considered alone, the value of F for each cleavage would be based on the portion crystallized on that cleavage. Here, though, since we wish to use the results of section 4.3 on the relations between XC and (F_1, F_2), the values of F must be based on the individuals in the overlap between X_1 and X_2. Fortunately, the overlap C^h is usually very high for trait cleavages, so that these F values will be similar to those based on the separate crystallized portions.

Proposition 4': If both F_1 and F_2 are either too low or too high, then democratic political organization is not likely to be stable.

Suppose now that the amount of cross-cutting between these two cleavages is defined as XC—the measure introduced above. Then proposition 1, which was in effect a summary statement of the various explanations of democratic stability based on cross-cutting cleavages, may be rewritten as

Proposition 1': If the value of XC is too low, then democratic political organization is not likely to be stable.

Now, we have already seen that, when F_1 and F_2 are both high or both low, XC must be low. Thus proposition 4' implies proposition 1'. Propositions 1' and 4' and figures 4.6 and 4.7 may now be combined to produce fig. 4.8. The points A and B are those of fig. 4.7.

The curve in fig. 4.8 is the maximum cross-cutting which is possible for a given value of $F_1 (= F_2)$.[25] Since the minimum possible value of XC is zero when $F_1 = F_2$, fig. 4.8 shows that:

1. When both F_1 and F_2 are to the left of B or to the right of A, XC must be low.
2. When F_1 and F_2 lie between the points A and B, XC can have anything from zero to fairly high values.

Thus propositions 1' and 4' are not entirely equivalent. Proposition 1' does not imply proposition 4', since XC can be low when F_1 and F_2 are not both high or both low. But it is clear that these two theories of democratic stability are not independent: the amounts of fragmentation associated with the separate cleavages place bounds on the amount of cross-cutting which is possible.

25. The curve would be very similar in shape if F_1 and F_2 were only approximately equal.

Figure 4.8

The Relation Between Social Pluralism
and Cross-Cutting

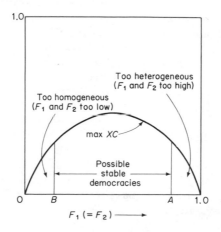

Intensity of fragmentation and intensity of conflict

The preceding discussion of social pluralism has been solely in terms of F and XC. With some of the trait cleavages with which this theory is concerned, the intensity of fragmentation (I) may be meaningless or unimportant. In the case of a trait cleavage like religion, however, it may become extremely important, since there will normally be considerable variation in the intensity with which individuals belong to religious groups. The impact of both the fragmentation and cross-cutting of cleavages upon democratic stability will be modified by these intensity variations, where they are applicable.

The word "intensity," however, is used by theorists of conflict and democratic stability not only to qualify an individual's memberships in nominal groups, but also to qualify the conflict between these groups. These two usages are quite distinct. Cross-cutting is said to reduce the intensity of conflict in the community. The cross-pressured individual, with memberships in several groups which pull him in different political directions, may reduce the intensity of his political commitment; his identification with a political party may become less intense. But his other group memberships may be held intensely; indeed, if they were not, he would be less cross-pressured. It is of course possible that he will reduce dissonance by withdrawing from some of his opposed groups or by reducing his commitment to them, while maintaining an intense political position.

In either case, although the intensity of group membership and the intensity of conflict are empirically related, they are quite distinct variables. The intensity of conflict depends on both the intensities of group memberships (the intensity ranks of chapter 3) and the amount of cross-cutting.[26] These are empirical relations and are outside the scope of this monograph. But we hope that our measures (F, I, and XC) will be of use in any future theory of democratic stability which takes into account both these empirical relations and the relations which we have shown to hold, by definition, between fragmentation and the amount of cross-cutting.

4.6 Summary

Throughout this chapter we have been concerned again with the formation of a concept through definition. Despite its importance in the study of politics, this concept— the cross-cutting of political cleavages— has not previously been given a precise definition. The explication offered here has led to a measure of cross-cutting which has a clear operational interpretation and which we hope will

26. The more the cleavages reinforce one another, the more intense the conflict will be.

be of use in empirical work in comparative politics. The cross-cutting (XC) of two cleavages was defined as the proportion of all the pairs of individuals whose two members are in the same group of one cleavage but in different groups of the other cleavage. It was demonstrated that complete cross-cutting cannot occur.

The relation between cross-cutting on the one hand and the fragmentation of the two cleavages on the other was explored, by first deriving the result $XC = 2F_c - F_1 - F_2$ and then seeing, through a series of examples, how F_1 and F_2 place bounds on the possible values of XC.

Other properties of the measure emerged from a comparison of XC with measures of statistical association, which in the past have sometimes been used in studies of cross-cutting.

Finally, we discussed the implications of the relations between F_1, F_2 and XC for theories of democratic stability. This, we hope, has illustrated the way in which concepts constrain theories.

APPENDIX A

OTHER MEASURES OF FRAGMENTATION
AT THE NOMINAL LEVEL

In this book, we have developed an approach to the analysis of cleavages at the nominal level of measurement: the groups (or alternatives) are distinguished only in qualitative terms. So we assume only that A_1 is different from A_2, not that one ranks higher on some ordination, or holds a higher value on some cardinal scale. In appendix B, we present alternative analyses which presume higher levels of measurement, but here we catalogue other measures of fragmentation (or its opposite— cohesion, for example) based on nominal alternatives.

Our basic index, fractionalization, is concerned with the degree to which a cleavage divides a community into different nominal groups (see chapter 2). Since this property of a cleavage is so important in so wide a variety of political processes, it is not surprising that many others have proposed measures for it. Since we have already given our argument for F, what remains is to catalogue these related measures and to offer a brief commentary on each. This annotated catalogue of other measures is presented under three broad headings: (1) those based on modal frequencies, (2) those based on pairwise relations (like F), and (3) those based on information theory.

A. 1 Modal Frequency Measures

The oldest and largest class of measures may be defined by its reliance upon the modal frequency. Here we answer the question, "How divided is this community?" by asking the simpler question, "How many of the members do not belong to the largest single group?" This response is appropriate wherever we can assume dichotomous cleavages for which n equals two— as in most voting bodies. But, since it necessarily puts aside all other alternatives, this approach is not general to n alternatives.

The Rice index of group cohesion

If one assumes that there are exactly two nominal groups — like the Ayes and Nays on a legislative vote — then a very simple definition is possible for the degree to which a group or community is divided. If most members are in one of the two alternatives, we have little division; if they are evenly split between the two, we have much division. This is the underlying assumption of Stuart Rice's index of group cohesion:

$$\text{Rice index score} = \frac{|f_1 - f_2|}{N} \cdot 100$$

This has values from 0 through 100. The index is simply the percentage difference between the more populous and the less populous of two alternative nominal groups (Rice 1925, 1949). If the members split equally between two alternatives, the index value is zero; if all members choose one alternative, the value is 100.

The resulting values have the virtue of simplicity and may be useful so long as there are exactly two alternatives. The Rice index has been applied with some success under such circumstances (Key 1949; Rieselbach 1960).

Index of relative cohesion

A still simpler and formally more general measure is simply the proportion of members who belong to the most popular of n alternatives:

$$\text{Index of relative cohesion} = \frac{f_{max}}{N}$$

This varies from 0 through 1.

If we suppose that half of 100 members belong to the most populous alternative, then the value of the index is

$50/100 = .5$. If all belong to one alternative, then it is $100/100 = 1.0$.

This measure, presented by Anderson and Watts (1965), has all the virtues and limitations of the Rice index. Its most important limitation is its failure to respond to the distribution of members among the less populous alternatives, so it too can be usefully applied only where there are exactly two alternatives ($n = 2$).

This intuitively appealing measure has a wide range of applications and modifications (Prothro and Grigg 1960; McCloskey 1964; Derge 1959). One not-too-helpful modification is the insertion of a cut-point, so that we say that a group exhibits cohesion or consensus or homogeneity above a certain index value and does not exhibit these qualities below that index value. For Prothro and Grigg, the cut-point is usually .9, while for McCloskey it is .75.[1] These cut-points waste information and do not simplify interpretation, although they are helpful for certain forms of tabular presentation.

Kalela's generalization

An attempt at a generalization of the measures just discussed begins with reasoning of the following sort: "If there are a few alternatives, then it is more likely that many people will adopt any one alternative; with more alternatives, this concentration seems less probable. We must therefore norm our measure for the number of alternatives." This is essentially what Jaakko Kalela (1967) suggests in the following index.

$$\text{Kalela's index} = \left(\frac{100}{100 - \dfrac{100}{n}}\right) \cdot \left(\frac{100}{N} \cdot f_{max} - \frac{100}{n}\right)$$

$$= \frac{n}{n-1} \cdot 100 \left(\frac{f_{max}}{N} - \frac{1}{n}\right)$$

1. Another approach is to compare modal frequencies between various cleavages and communities, resting one's cut-points on ordinations of modal frequencies. See Budge 1970.

This varies from 0 through 100. If there are two alternatives, and 50 out of 100 members adopt the most popular, the value is

$$\frac{2}{1} \cdot 100\left(\frac{50}{100} - \frac{1}{2}\right) = 0$$

But if we have three alternatives, and 50 out of 100 members adopt the most popular, the value is

$$\frac{3}{2} \cdot 100\left(\frac{50}{100} - \frac{1}{3}\right) = 25$$

Similarly, if we have five alternatives with the same modal frequency (i.e., 50), the index would reach 37.5.

We may interpret Kalela's measure as a normed deviation from the even distribution of members over n alternatives. That is, the measure equals zero when and only when the modal frequency (f_{max}) is exactly $1/N$ and, by implication, all other frequencies are also equal to $1/N$. Its upper bound occurs when all members are in the modal frequency, $f_{max} = N$. But, between these two bounds, no useful theoretical interpretation may be offered. This is because the index is sensitive only to one frequency in relation to the number of frequencies (i.e., alternatives) and does not capture the distribution of members over the remaining $n - 1$ alternatives.

Galtung's measure of nominal dispersion

Another use of the modal frequency is offered by Johan Galtung's (1967) measure of nominal dispersion. This measure follows if we begin by asking, "What is missing from the modal frequency relative to what could in principle be missing?" Since the mode must have a frequency of at least one, the maximum sum of nonmodal frequencies is $N - 1$, and we divide this into the actual nonmodal frequency ($N - f_{max}$) to obtain the index value.

Galtung's index of
nominal dispersion $= \dfrac{N - f_{max}}{N - 1}$

This varies from 0 through 1.

If each of 100 members takes a separate alternative, we obtain a value of one; if all 100 take a single alternative, we obtain a dispersion value of zero.

This measure has all the faults of the measures discussed above, and the additional liability of unnecessary complexity. With Galtung's index, and all its simpler alternatives, the modal frequency captures too little information.

A. 2 Pairwise Agreement Measures

A second general class of measures is much more closely related to F as we have defined it, for these measures are defined in terms of pairwise agreement. In general, these measures are products of research on voting bodies and are defined for two alternatives— Aye and Nay. Some add a third alternative, abstention. And each may be understood as a special case or close relative of F.

Pairwise agreement

A very simple approach begins by defining what amounts to the complement of F over two alternatives and considering it an index of cohesion. The two alternatives represent Aye and Nay votes.

$$\text{Cohesion} = \dfrac{\substack{\text{number of pairs} \\ \text{saying Aye}} + \substack{\text{number of pairs} \\ \text{saying Nay}}}{\text{total number of pairs}}$$

This, obviously, is a special case of F, where we have two labeled alternatives and, since we are measuring cohesion rather than division, do not take the complement of the fraction.

Voting concordance

A variant of the same scheme occurs when we add a third alternative, for paired abstention:

$$\text{Voting concordance} = \frac{\begin{array}{c}\text{number of} \\ \text{pairs} \\ \text{abstaining}\end{array} + \begin{array}{c}\text{number of} \\ \text{pairs} \\ \text{voting Aye}\end{array} + \begin{array}{c}\text{number of} \\ \text{pairs} \\ \text{voting Nay}\end{array}}{\text{total number of pairs}}$$

This index takes abstention into account by treating it as the formal equivalent of Aye and Nay voting. In this respect, it differs from F, which treats abstention under the concept of crystallization and omits its frequency from the computation. This index is best known for its use in analyses of the U.N. General Assembly (Jacobson 1967).

Both of the above measures have the universe of pairs interpretation given in the present work for F. And both are restricted to two or three alternative applications. Another variant loses this theoretical interpretation without adding generality.

Pairwise solidarity

Another measure begins by defining two forms of agreement: (1) ordinary agreement in which case both members of a pair cast the same (Aye or Nay) vote, and (2) "solidarity pairs," where one member cast such a vote and the other abstained. The first class of pairs count for a full agreement; the latter for half an agreement. The result is as follows.

$$\text{Solidarity} = \frac{\begin{array}{c}\text{number of} \\ \text{pairs} \\ \text{voting Aye}\end{array} + \begin{array}{c}\text{number of} \\ \text{pairs} \\ \text{voting Nay}\end{array} + \frac{1}{2}\left(\begin{array}{c}\text{number of} \\ \text{solidarity} \\ \text{pairs}\end{array}\right)}{\text{total number of pairs}}$$

This index offers a sort of compromise treatment for abstention, but there is no simple interpretation of its values. Why should solidarity pairs be counted exactly one-half? While ad hoc measures of this kind may be useful to specific analyses, they hold little promise for theoretical development. For applications of this index, see Lijphart (1963) or Lidstrom and Wiklund (1967).

F-like measures

The measure defined in chapter 2, fragmentation, or its complement, has been used outside political science. (These uses were discovered only after the present work was nearly completed.) The reader may wish to consult Simpson (1949), Greenberg (1956), or Hall and Tideman (1967) for applications in other fields. These measures have simple though varied theoretical interpretations in their respective contexts. And only the "political" interpretation given here is novel.

Other measures of pairwise agreement

A variety of other measures, usually designed for some specific context, have used pairwise agreement relations to define cohesion or fragmentation. Most of these measures deal with series of roll-call votes and interest themselves in the number of votes on which a given pair of members agreed or disagreed. The most current source on these measures is Brams and O'Leary (1968).

A. 3 Information-Theoretic Measures

Other measures—namely those with logarithmic terms—are loosely associated with information theory, and more particularly with the concept of entropy. As Shannon and Weaver (1964) put it, "the entropy associated with a situation is a measure of the degree of randomness, or of 'shuffledness' if you will." Such measures promise, at least, a high level of generality, although there seems to be some confusion about their interpretation.

Galtung's information theoretic measure

Galtung (1967) proposes a measure of uncertainty which is, in fact, equivalent to the definition used by the information theorists for "entropy."[2]

2. In information theory, the base 2 is used to represent binary choices in communication.

$$\text{Uncertainty} = -\sum_{i=1}^{n} \left(\frac{f_i}{N}\right) \log_2\left(\frac{f_i}{N}\right)$$

This may have values from zero to infinity.

Like F and its relatives, this quantity is sensitive to both the number and the relative equality of the frequencies: the more equal the frequencies, the higher the index value. Even noting the indeterminacy of the measure's upper bound, it is preferable to many of the alternatives noted above, for it is general to n alternatives.

Kesselman's multipartism measure

A related measure is offered by Kesselman (1966). In his analysis of French local elections, Kesselman used this index to represent the extent to which election choices divided the electors of various districts.

$$\text{Multipartism} = \text{antilog}_e \left\{ -\sum_{i=1}^{n} \left(\frac{f_i}{N}\right) \log_e \left(\frac{f_i}{N}\right) \right\}$$

This index is also sensitive both to the number and relative equality of frequencies (i.e., party shares of the vote). Unhappily, the author gives no general interpretation for the resulting values. Any straightforward information-theoretic interpretation seems to be precluded by the antilog term and by the use of logs to the base e (≈ 2.71).

APPENDIX B: MEASURES OF CONSENSUS FOR ORDINAL AND INTERVAL DATA

B. 1 Introduction

Throughout the main part of this book we have considered only the case in which the alternatives are assumed to be measured at the nominal level. Our reasons were given in chapter 1 for believing that stronger assumptions cannot often be made with full confidence, and that, in any case, the division of a community into mere groups is politically the most important aspect of the cleavage. However, it is sometimes the case that we have more information about the alternatives and wish to assume that they are, for instance, ordered in one dimension or separated by approximately equal intervals.

A case in which assumptions about the intervals between alternatives might reasonably be made is one in which the alternatives are various amounts for an appropriation—although even here there are complications, as the following example shows. Suppose the alternatives were $1, $2, $3, $4, $5 (or multiples thereof). Each individual chooses his most preferred alternative, and we wish to measure the consensus among these individuals. Any measure (such as those in section B.3 below) based on the assumption that the alternatives are equally spaced (as indeed they appear to be) must proceed by saying, for example, that two individuals, one choosing $1 and the other choosing $5, are four times as "disagreed" as two individuals choosing $1 and $2, since they are four times as far apart on the assumed scale on which the alternatives are positioned. (This is, in fact, the basis for both the measures in section B.4.) But it may be that the individual who most prefers to see $1 appropriated would next prefer $5. This preference schedule would probably reflect the dependence, in his view, of this issue on others. The individual might think, "Let us spend all, or nothing;

123

let us do this thing properly, or not at all." Thus it is not always the case that disagreement between two individuals increases as some distance between them increases.

This example should show that such assumptions, when used as the basis for a measure of consensus, are very strong indeed. We seem to be making an assumption about only the alternatives, whereas in reality we are also making an assumption about the individuals' preferences. We can, of course, ask the individual for his whole preference schedule, perhaps by asking him to rank all the alternatives. (Measures of consensus among such rankings are discussed below, in section B.4.) But in the case when each individual states only his most preferred alternative, then if, for example, a measure assumes that the alternatives are ordered, it must always be interpreted as consensus with respect to that particular ordering.

Having made these cautionary remarks (which cannot be overemphasized and should be borne in mind throughout this appendix), we now present several measures of consensus, based on alternatives measured at the ordinal and interval levels. Strictly speaking, they may be used in connection with all three types of cleavage, but the word "consensus" is retained, partly because some of these measures have originated elsewhere, with this or a similar label, and partly because these stronger assumptions about the alternatives are more often appropriate in the case of opinion cleavages.

B. 2 Ordinal Consensus

Simple ordinal consensus

First, we consider the measurement of consensus in the case when the choice alternatives are assumed to be ordered, and each individual merely chooses one alternative without expressing the intensity of his preference. For convenience we shall refer to this type of consensus, which takes the assumed ordering into account, as simple ordinal consensus.

Sometimes the assumption of an ordering of the alternatives is unquestionable: the ordering suggests itself naturally, as when the alternatives are merely quantities or degrees of the same thing. The assumption, frequent in the past, that political parties are ordered along a single liberal–conservative continuum is being increasingly challenged: the parties must be positioned, not along one dimension, but in a space of several dimensions; and even this would be of value only if all the voters (for example) perceived the parties to lie in this same space.[1] Another example was discussed at the end of section 3.1, where it was argued that degrees of agreement and disagreement (from "agree strongly" through "indifference" to "disagree," for example) are not always ordered along a single dimension, as is commonly assumed.

If, however, an ordering is assumed, and we wish to use this fact in a measure of consensus without making any assumptions about the intervals between alternatives, then we might proceed as follows.

Whatever the type of ordering, the data can be presented graphically in the form of a histogram. The alternatives (A_i) are ordered as abscissae (relabeling, if necessary, so that the ordering is $A_1, A_2, \ldots, A_n$), and the ordinate corresponding to A_i is the number of individuals, f_i, who choose A_i. As a means of depicting the data, such diagrams may be helpful, but for use in comparing two sets of data they are only suggestive—and may be misleading.

Fortunately, an excellent measure of consensus for this type of data has already been developed. This measure, proposed by Robert Leik (1966, pp. 85–90), is based upon the assumptions made above: the alternatives are merely ordered, and each individual chooses one alternative. We follow Leik closely in presenting this measure but use our own notations.

1. Cf. Stokes 1963, pp. 368–77, and Converse (chapter 9 in Jennings and Zeigler 1966). Converse used Coombs's Unfolding Technique on samples of French and Finnish voters and showed that, in each case, their preferences were not consistent with a single ordering of the parties.

As before the frequency distribution of choices among the n alternatives A_1, A_2, . . . , A_n is f_1, f_2, . . . , f_n. The relative frequencies (A_i/N), where N is the total number of individuals, are now cumulated to produce the cumulative relative frequency distribution (CF_i), where

$$CF_i = \frac{1}{N} \sum_{j \leq i} f_j$$

We now define a difference, d_i, equal to CF_i if $CF_i \leq 1/2$, and $1 - CF_i$ otherwise. It will be seen that, in the case of maximum consensus (i.e., zero dispersion, when all N individuals choose the same alternative), $d_i = 0$ for all i, no matter which alternative is chosen. Suppose n = 6, and the one alternative which is chosen is A_4. Then the relative frequencies are (0, 0, 0, 1, 0, 0), so that the cumulative relative frequencies F_i are (0, 0, 0, 1, 1, 1). Hence the d_i are all zero; and

$$\sum_{i=1}^{n} d_i = 0$$

for the zero dispersion case. Maximum dispersion occurs when all the choices are divided evenly between the two most extreme alternatives; that is, $f_i = N/2$ for i = 1 and i = n, and $f_i = 0$ for all other i. In this case the f_i are (1/2, 1/2, . . . , 1/2, 1), so that the d_i are (1/2, 1/2, . . . , 1/2, 0). Hence $d_i = 1/2(n-1)$. For n alternatives this is the maximum value of d_i. So

$$D = \frac{\sum d_i}{\max \sum d_i} = \frac{2 \sum d_i}{n-1}$$

is used as a measure of dispersion. "Simple ordinal consensus" is then defined as $C_1 = 1 - D$; that is,

$$C_1 = 1 - \frac{2 \sum_{i=1}^{n} d_i}{n-1}$$

Computing the value of C_1 for a few different sets of data will convince the reader how accurately it measures the amount of consensus. C_1 uses only the information that the alternatives are ordered; it does not depend for a meaningful interpretation on any further requirements, such as the assumption that the intervals between alternatives are equal. C_1 is independent of N and n; hence it may be used to compare sets of data using different numbers of choice alternatives. Its maximum value, when all individuals choose the same alternative, is one. Its minimum value, when all the choices are evenly divided between the two most extreme alternatives, is zero. In the case which we have previously called a "uniform distribution," where $f_i = N/n$ for all i, C_1 is found to depend on n, varying from .33 at n = 3 through .44 at n = 10 and approaching .50 as n tends to infinity.[2] It should not alarm us that the value of C_1 for this distribution (which is the distribution resulting from a random choice of alternatives by each individual) varies with n; we have already seen the same phenomenon with the measure of fragmentation F. Leik notes that if n = 2, then the uniform distribution case ($f_{ij} = N/2$ for i = 1, 2) is identical with the maximum dispersion case. We would go further and say that a measure of ordinal consensus is inapplicable where there are only two alternatives, since any ordering of two things is purely arbitrary. Rather, the data should be treated as though there were two nominal alternatives, and the measure of fragmentation F used.

The definition of consensus given above did not, of course, use the framework developed in the main part of the book. The set of pairs of individuals could have been divided between mixed and matched pairs, and the mixed pairs further distributed according to how many alternatives separate their two members, but a measure of consensus using this approach would require an assumption that the alternatives were equally spaced.

Intensities in ordinal consensus

We shall now define a measure of consensus which takes into account the intensities with which individuals

2. See Leik 1966, p. 87.

cleave to their positions — their most preferred alternative. Since we have not followed the approach used in the main part of the book, this measure will not be complementary to C_1 (as I was to F); rather, it will replace C_1 whenever intensities are to be used. All the remarks on the concept of intensity in section 3.1 are relevant here also.

We use the same notation as in section 3.2, remembering, however, that the n alternatives (A_i) are now ordered. Initially, we assume that the m intensity ranks (R_i) are only ordered. Suppose that, with relabeling if necessary, these two orders are (A_1, A_2, . . . , A_n) and (R_1, R_2, . . . , R_m). Let f_{ij} be the number of individuals choosing alternative A_j at intensity rank R_i. The data can be arrayed in a matrix, as before.

$$
\begin{array}{c}
 \\
(order) \\
\xrightarrow{\hspace{2cm}}
\end{array}
$$

		A_1	A_2		A_j		A_n
	R_1	f_{11}	f_{12} $\cdots$	$\cdot$		$\cdots$	f_{1n}
	R_2	f_{21}	f_{22} $\cdots$	$\cdot$		$\cdots$	f_{2n}
	$\cdot$	$\cdot$	$\cdot$ $\cdots$	$\cdot$		$\cdots$	$\cdot$
R_i		$\cdot$	$\cdot$ $\cdots$		f_{ij}	$\cdots$	$\cdot$
(order)							
	$\cdot$	$\cdot$	$\cdot$ $\cdots$	$\cdot$		$\cdots$	$\cdot$
	R_m	f_{m1}	f_{m2} $\cdots$	$\cdot$		$\cdots$	f_{mn}

Two approaches to a definition of consensus suggest themselves. The first approach is analogous to that followed for the intensity of fragmentation (section 3.2). We could define a distance, d, between an individual at (R_{i_1}, A_{j_1}) and an individual at (R_{i_2}, A_{j_2}) as

$$d = i_1 + i_2 + \left| j_2 - j_1 \right| \tag{B.1}$$

so that the more intense either individual is, the greater is d; and the further apart the two chosen alternatives are, the greater is d. The maximum value of d would occur when the two individuals choose the two most extreme alternatives at the most extreme intensity rank. As before, we would derive the probability P_d that two individuals drawn at random are separated by a distance d for each value of d. Consensus would then be defined as a sum of weighted P_d's.

There are two reasons for not adopting this approach. First, the resulting formula and its derivation are complicated, and, worse yet, the formula is not easy to use, even for quite small values of m and n. Second, and far more damning, the formula is only plausible as a measure of consensus if further assumptions are made about the data. For distances along the intensity ranks to have any meaning, the intervals between the ranks must be equal; similarly, the intervals between alternatives must be equal. Furthermore, these two distances must be comparable in some way—for instance, by assuming that intervals between alternatives are equal to those between intensity ranks. Note that formally this can be avoided: by replacing equation (B.1) with a definition of d in terms of the number of ranks separating two individuals, we do not have to assign numbers to ranks and then perform arithmetic operations on the numbers. But as a measure of consensus the formula would have little meaning without the additional assumptions, which in sum demand that all the intervals in the matrix are equal. These are very strong assumptions.

The second approach to be followed here is a generalization of Leik's measure for simple ordinal consensus. In computing the amount of dispersion of choices, the contribution of each individual will be weighted according to the intensity with which he makes his choice: the more intense his choice, the greater his contribution to the dispersion. We do not have to weight individuals separately, however; there is a simple way of computing the new dispersion D as follows. In terms of the formulation given above, the frequencies (f_i) used by Leik are the column sums of the matrix (f_{ij}) shown above. That is,

$$f_i = \sum_{s=1}^{m} f_{si}$$

If we weight each individual's contribution to D by the number of his intensity rank $(1, 2, \ldots,$ or $m)$, then the f_i used by Leik must be replaced by f'_i defined as follows:

$$f'_i = \sum_{s=1}^{m} s \cdot f_{si}$$

Thus, for example, if the matrix is

$$\begin{bmatrix} 2 & 2 & 3 \\ 1 & 7 & 0 \end{bmatrix}$$

then the f'_i are found to be $(4, 16, 3)$. These new frequencies are now treated as though they were in fact an ordinal frequency distribution of the sort considered by Leik, and the remainder of the derivation of the consensus measure proceeds exactly as the derivation given above for simple ordinal consensus. Thus the f'_i are converted to relative frequencies by dividing each of them by

$$\sum_{i=1}^{n} f'_i = N'$$

and then cumulated to obtain CF'_i, where

$$CF'_i = \frac{1}{N'} \sum_{j \leq i} f'_j$$

A difference d'_i is defined as equal to CF'_i if $CF'_i \leq 1/2$ and $1 - CF'_i$ otherwise; and "consensus" is defined as

$$C_2 = 1 - \frac{\sum_{i=1}^{n} d'_i}{\max d'_i}$$

In this case, maximum dispersion occurs when all the individuals are evenly divided between the extreme intensities of the two extreme alternatives; that is, when $f_{ij} = N/2$ for $i = m$ and $j = 1$ or n, and $f_{ij} = 0$ otherwise. Maximum dispersion is found to be $(n-1)/2$, as before; so that we have

$$C_2 = 1 - \frac{2 \sum_{i=1}^{n} d'_i}{n-1}$$

131

Maximum consensus occurs when all individuals choose the same alternative, regardless of the distribution of their choices over the intensity ranks. In this case it is found that the cumulative frequencies (CF'_i), when the rows of F are weighted $1, 2, \ldots, m$, are $(1, 1, \ldots, 1)$. Hence $d'_i = 0$ for all i, and so $C_2 = 1$.

The effect of taking intensities into account can be seen in the following simple examples.

1. First, suppose our data consisted only of the simple ordinal distribution $(f_i) = (3, 9, 3)$. Then we find $C_1 = .60$.

2. Now suppose the data are

$$\begin{bmatrix} 2 & 2 & 3 \\ 1 & 7 & 0 \end{bmatrix}$$

   where the column sums are $(3, 9, 3)$ — the same as the distribution in (1). Using C_2, with weights $(1, 2)$, we find $C_2 = .69$. Thus the high intensity of the center choices and the low intensity of the neighboring choices cause a very substantial increase in consensus.

3. Suppose now that we are able to obtain data with three intensity ranks:

$$\begin{bmatrix} 2 & 0 & 3 \\ 1 & 2 & 0 \\ 0 & 7 & 0 \end{bmatrix}$$

   — again with the same marginal frequencies $(3, 9, 3)$ as in (1) and (2). C_2 is found to be .78 — the same effect as in (2), taken further.

4. Now consider a situation of less consensus, where the extreme choices (those for A_1 and A_3) are very intense, and the center choices (A_2) are weak:

$$\begin{bmatrix} 0 & 9 & 0 \\ 0 & 0 & 0 \\ 3 & 0 & 3 \end{bmatrix}$$

132

— again with the same marginal frequencies. Here, $C_2 = .33$, which represents a considerable drop in consensus, as required.

Returning now to the assumptions upon which this measure is based, we note first that the assignment of weights to the intensity ranks is purely arbitrary. Secondly, this assignment implies an assumption about the intervals between the ranks. However, the weights which we have chosen to use (namely 1, 2, . . . , m) are fully justified if no more is assumed than that the intervals between intensity ranks are equal; and it will be seen that any set of weights based on this assumption (e.g., 3, 6, 9, . . . , 3m) will lead to precisely the same values for C_2. Of course, C_2 may always be used for this type of data, but the degree to which it is a reasonable measure of consensus will depend on the degree to which the intervals between the intensity ranks are in fact equal. As with all indices, then, caution should be exercised in the use of C_2.

B. 3 Interval Consensus

In the preceding section we have presented indices of consensus for distributions where it is assumed only that the alternatives are ordered. Sometimes, though, one may wish to make stronger assumptions about the scale on which the alternatives lie. For instance, if the choice alternatives are amounts of money for a budgetary appropriation, we can measure the intervals between alternatives quite naturally. In fig. B.1 for example, if the intervals are comparable in the way indicated, then clearly the upper distribution has more consensus than the lower, even though the actual relative frequency distributions are identical. In cases like this where stronger assumptions seem justified, we would lose a lot of information if we measured consensus with C_1.

Two measures of consensus, based on stronger assumptions than have been made thus far, will be discussed.

133

The first measure depends on the assumption of equal intervals between alternatives; the second is related to the variance of the distribution and thus also requires an interval level of measurement of the alternatives but not equal intervals. The data are, of course, no different in appearance than they were for simple ordinal consensus; that is, each individual chooses one and only one from among n alternatives. The difference is that we wish to construct an index which is capable of reflecting the equality of, or differences in, the sizes of intervals between alternatives.

Consensus as the complement of average pairwise disagreement

The first measure of interval consensus requires the assumption that the intervals between alternatives are equal. For any set of data it will produce the same values for any assignment of numbers to the intervals, providing all intervals are given the same number. We shall, therefore, simplify the index in advance by assuming that the intervals are all of unit length.

Figure B. 1

Two Distributions With Identical Frequencies

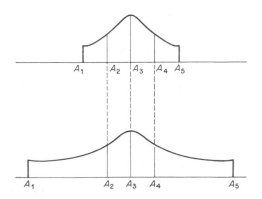

134

Denote the positions of the alternatives A_1, A_2, . . . , A_n on this interval scale by x_1, x_2, . . . , x_n; that is, x_i is the distance of A_i from an arbitrary origin. Assume that, relabeling the alternatives if necessary, $x_1 < x_2 < . . . < x_n$. Let f_i be the number of individuals choosing A_i, as before. Figure B.2 shows an example (where no assumptions need be made about the distance Ox_1).

Figure B.2

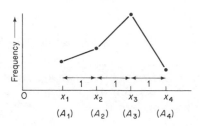

"Consensus" will now be defined as the complement of the average pairwise difference of choice. First, the choice difference (or, in appropriate contexts, the difference of opinion) between the ith and j^{th} individuals is $|x^{(i)} - x^{(j)}|$, where $x^{(i)}$ denotes the x-value of the alternative chosen by the ith individual. The total number of pairs of different individuals (with no regard for their order) in a set of N individuals is $2\binom{N}{2}$, or $N(N-1)$. Hence, the mean pairwise difference for the whole set is shown in expression (B.2).[3]

$$\sum_{i,\,j=1}^{N} |x^{(i)} - x^{(j)}|$$ (B.2)

3. The summation can be performed over all values of i and j, since $|x^{(i)} - x^{(j)}| = 0$ if $i = j$. Note that every pair is counted twice in the summation, but their difference will be the same in each case, and they are also counted twice in the denominator.

If the number of alternatives is n, then the maximum possible pairwise difference is $(n-1)$, since we have assumed unit intervals. Hence to further "normalize" expression (B.2), we divide by $(n-1)$, which gives the dispersion divided by its maximum value, D. Consensus, C_3, is then defined as the complement of this dispersion. Thus

$$C_3 = 1 - \frac{1}{N(N-1)(n-1)} \sum_{i,j=1}^{N} \left| x^{(j)} - x^{(i)} \right|$$

and $0 \le C \le 1$. Maximum consensus ($C_3 = 1$) occurs when all individuals choose the same alternative; minimum consensus occurs when the individuals are equally divided between the alternatives at the two extremes. In this case, the only nonzero contributions to D are when $x^{(j)}$ is an A_1 choice and $x^{(i)}$ is an A_n choice, or vice versa, and these contributions will be each $n-1$. Hence we find

$$\max D = \frac{N}{2(N-1)}$$

Thus as $N \to \infty$, $\max D \to 1/2$. Max D is in fact very close to $1/2$ for the range of values of N which are most likely to be encountered. C_3 is zero, then, only when $N = 2$; and, under this definition, the minimum value of C_3 is normally quite high—approximately $1/2$. This is not as alarming as might appear at first sight: it is a reflection of the fact that, when the total set of individuals is split between the two extremes, there is complete consensus within each of these two factions. There can only be complete disagreement between two individuals. Caution must therefore be exercised in using C_3 to compare systems with different numbers of alternatives.

When N is large the computation of all pairwise differences would be very tedious. But if the frequencies (f_i) are known (as they are, for instance, after the usual survey analysis), there is an equivalent definition of C_3 which is very simple to use. Its derivation is as follows.

The contributions to the numerator of D of all pairs of individuals such that one is at A_i and the other is at

A_{i+s} are each s. Thus the total contribution of such pairs (disregarding order within pairs) is

$$2s \sum_{i=1}^{n-s} f_i f_{i+s}$$

Summing over all possible values of s, and dividing by the total number of pairs and by the maximum possible pairwise difference $(n-1)$, as before, we have

$$D = \frac{\sum_{s=1}^{n-1} s \sum_{i=1}^{n-s} f_i f_{i+s}}{N(N-1)(n-1)}$$

and we define C_3 as equal to $1-D$.

The two definitions are entirely equivalent, but the second one enables C_3 to be computed by hand very simply from the frequency distribution.

Consensus as the complement of variance

The second measure of interval consensus, proposed by Leik and analogous to his measure of simple ordinal consensus, is based on variance of the distribution of choices.[4]

Variance measures require, of course, an interval level of measurement; that is, we must be able to assign real numbers to the intervals between alternatives. We no longer assume that these intervals are equal. Denote the positions of the alternatives A_1, A_2, . . . , A_n on this interval scale by x_1, x_2, . . . , x_n, so that x_i denotes the distance of A_i from some arbitrary origin. Assume that, relabeling if necessary, $x_1 < x_2 < . . . < x_n$. It is possible here that n is quite large; for example, each individual may be allowed to choose any sum of money (within some specified range) which he thinks should comprise a certain ap-

---

4. Leik 1966; see also Axelrod 1968. Axelrod has started from assumptions about the utilities of a set of choice alternatives in bargaining games and arrived at a measure of conflict of interest as the variance, s^2, of the distribution of choices, as defined below.

propriation. Let the alternative chosen by the ith individual be $x^{(i)}$. Then the usual statistical measure of variance is defined in equation (B.3).

$$s^2 = \frac{1}{N} \sum_{j=1}^{N} (x^{(j)} - \bar{x})^2, \tag{B.3}$$

where N is the total number of individuals, as before, and $\bar{x}$ is the mean of all the $x^{(j)}$'s. If f_i is the number of individuals choosing the alternative A_i, then this can also be written:

$$s^2 = \frac{1}{N} \sum_{i=1}^{n} f_i (x_i - \bar{x})^2$$

For a measure of dispersion, normed so as to be independent of the number of alternatives, we use $s^2 / \max s^2$. The maximum value of s^2 occurs when all the individuals are divided equally between the two extreme alternatives, in which case the mean $\bar{x}$ is at zero, and x_1 and x_n are each at a distance of $(x_n - x_1)/2$ from the mean. Thus

$$\max s^2 = \left(\frac{x_n - x_1}{2}\right)^2$$

If the alternatives are at equal intervals, then we take the intervals to be each unity, and

$$\max s^2 = \left(\frac{n-1}{2}\right)^2$$

The second measure of interval consensus is now defined as the complement of this normalized variance.

$$C_4 = 1 - \frac{s^2}{\max s^2}$$

$$= 1 - \frac{4 \sum_{i=1}^{n} f_i (x_i - \bar{x})^2}{N(x_n - x_1)^2}$$

This measure can be generalized to take account of intensities by weighing each individual's contribution to the variance in equation (B.3) with his intensity. Denoting by $y^{(j)}$ the intensity with which the jth individual cleaves to his position, equation (B.3) would be replaced by

$$s^2 = \frac{1}{N} \sum_{j=1}^{N} (x^{(j)} - \bar{x})^2 \cdot y^{(j)}$$

The number (integer) of j's intensity rank may be $y^{(j)}$, but this could be a noninteger if intensity were measured at a higher level. Consensus would again be defined as $1 - (s^2/\max s^2)$.

B.4 Consensus Among Preference Rankings

In this section we shall discuss measures of consensus using a different type of data than hitherto. Previously, the data have been of the form in which each individual chooses one and only one alternative from some set of alternatives. Now, however, it is assumed that each individual states his preferences among all the available choice alternatives, but no assumptions are made about the alternatives themselves.

Fortunately, a good deal of work has been done on the problem of measuring agreement between rankings, mostly by Kendall and Babington Smith (see Kendall 1962), whose coefficients of concordance and agreement will now be discussed. As far as we know, these two coefficients have not previously been used with political data as measures of consensus, nor have such applications been suggested. It should be remembered that the coefficients— especially that of concordance— were developed mostly with a view toward measuring the correlation between various "attributes" or "criteria" by which a set of objects or individuals are ranked. In the present context, on the other hand, we are interested in the consensus among individuals, each of whom rank some set of alternatives which may or may not be persons (e.g., they may be alternative policies, or candidates in an election).

Our purpose here is not to give an exhaustive treatment of these coefficients, but to introduce them as potentially useful measures of consensus in political science.

Finally, a special type of consensus, of importance in the study of collective decisions, will be discussed.

The coefficient of concordance

It is assumed that each individual ranks all the alternatives A_1, A_2, . . . , A_n in a partial order of preference. By a "partial order" of the set (A_i), we mean a reflexive, transitive, antisymmetric relation defined on (A_i). The assumption of transitivity means that if A_i is preferred to A_j and A_j to A_k, then A_i is preferred to A_k, for all i, j, k. Thus each individual ranks the alternatives, possibly expressing indifference between some of them. We represent an individual's preference ranking as a vector; for example, $(A_4, A_1 - A_3, A_2)$ means that A_4 is most preferred, A_1 is tied with A_3 at the next rank, and A_2 is least preferred. Alternatively, the whole set of individual rankings will be displayed by placing against each alternative the rank assigned to it by each individual, as in table B.1, for example. Table B.1 contains hypothetical data; it represents the preference rankings of five alternatives by six individuals (n = 5, N = 6). For instance, the first individual's preference ranking is $(A_2, A_4, A_1, A_3, A_5)$.

Table B.1

Alternatives

		1	2	3	4	5
Individual	1	3	1	4	2	5
	2	5	2	3	4	1
	3	4	1	2	3	5
	4	5	3	1	2	4
	5	5	2	4	1	3
	6	3	1	5	2	4
Sum of ranks		25	10	19	14	22

Examples of possible alternatives are as follows: policies being considered by a legislature (here an explicit ordering of alternatives by each member is not given, although it may be possible to infer such orderings from the voting on various amendments, as in some cases Riker [1965] has done); alternative motions before a committee; the list of candidates in an election. The data (that is, the set of individual rankings) could, of course, arise as responses to survey questions; for example, each respondent may be asked to state his preferences on some local issue by ranking the various proposals currently being urged in the community.

If there are only two individuals (N = 2), then the measures of rank correlation available in the statistical literature would be appropriate measures of consensus. These are Kendall's tau and Spearman's rho. Since these two measures are well known, this special case will not be discussed here.[5] For larger values of N, the so-called coefficient of concordance would seem to be highly appropriate as a measure of consensus.[6] It is derived as follows. Consider the sum of ranks assigned by the individuals—for example, those shown in the last row of table B.1. If there were perfect consensus among the N individuals, then one alternative would receive N ranks of 1, so its sum of ranks would have been N; the next most favored alternative would receive N ranks of 2, so its total would be N; and so on. In general, if there is perfect consensus, the sums of ranks are N, 2N, 3N, . . . , nN (not necessarily in that order), where n is the number of alternatives. If, on the other hand, there was little consensus, then the sums of ranks would be approximately the same for each alternative. Thus a measure of consensus should be related to the variance among the n sums of ranks.

5. Rho and tau are fully discussed by Kendall 1962, and Siegel 1956.

6. The remainder of this subsection is based on Kendall 1962, chapter 6.

The sums of ranks themselves sum to $Nn(n+1)/2$, since they consist of a sum of N sets, each of which is the sum of the first n natural numbers. The mean value of the sum is therefore $N(n+1)/2$. In the data in table B.1 the sum of rank sums is 90, and the mean is 18. Consider the deviations about this mean. In our example these are 7, −8, 1, −4, 4. If there is perfect consensus (all rankings identical), the deviations of the rank sums are $-N(n-1)/2, -N(n-3)/2, \ldots, +N(n-1)/2$, though not necessarily in that order. The sum of the squares of these deviations is $N^2(n^3-n)/12$, which represents the maximum possible value of the sum of squared deviations.

Denoting by S the sum of squares of the actual deviations, Kendall and Babington Smith define

$$W = \frac{12S}{N^2(n^3-n)}$$

which is called the "coefficient of concordance."[7] W varies between 0 and 1. In our example (table B.1), we find S = 146, and hence W = .406. Unlike our previous measures of consensus, W has already enjoyed considerable use, and we shall therefore continue to use the label W and the term "concordance" rather than "consensus." It is emphasized again that we are using W here as a measure of consensus among individuals, not as a measure of correlation between attributes.

Kendall has drawn our attention to the fact that a zero or very low value of W may arise in essentially two different ways.[8] First, when the set of individuals is equally divided between two opposite rankings (one exactly the reverse of the other), the sums of ranks will be the same for all alternatives, and so W = 0. But although W = 0, there is yet a considerable community of preference, for each of the two subgroups is completely agreed. Second, a zero

7. If any of the rankings contain ties, as we have allowed, the formula for W has to be modified. For the details, see Kendall 1962, sections 6.6, 6.7.

8. See Kendall 1962, section 6.15.

value of N may also arise when there is no community of preference whatsoever. This is when the sums of ranks are all equal (so that $W = 0$), but there are no large subsets of the individuals who have high consensus, it corresponds to a uniform distribution of preference rankings.

Thus when an opinion is complex, in the sense that it consists of a whole preference ranking, severe dissensus is possible in a variety of ways. Clearly, though, these two types of zero consensus may have different implications for action. For example, in the opposed factions case, if one faction is slightly larger than the other (W will still be very small), then that faction may defeat the smaller faction in a series of votes; whereas in the uniform distribution case, a certain kind of deadlock may occur. We shall briefly return to this problem in the discussion of collective decisions below.

The coefficient of agreement[9]

It may be the case, however, that our data consist of so-called paired comparisons of the alternatives — where each possible pair of choice alternatives is presented to the individual, one pair at a time, and he states his preference for one member of the pair over the other. Such data may have been obtained because it was thought that the alternatives would be too complex to be ranked by the individual on a single dimension, or that such rankings would be unreliable. It is possible, then, that an individual be inconsistent in his choices; that is, his preferences may be intransitive.

The paired-comparison preferences of N individuals may be summarized in matrix form, as follows. We define a matrix B whose $(i, j)^{th}$ element, b_{ij}, is the number of individuals who prefer A_i to A_j. Each element is then some number from 0 to N. The number of possible pairs of alternative n is $\binom{n}{2}$, or $n(n-1)/2$. If there is com-

9. For a full discussion see Kendall 1962, chapters 11−12.

plete consensus among the N individuals, the matrix will contain $n(n-1)/2$ elements equal to N, the other half of the $n(n-1)$ elements of the matrix being zero. (The matrix contains no diagonal elements, of course.) The number b_{ij} may be thought of as being the number of individuals who agree that A_i is preferable to A_j. Thus $\binom{b_{ij}}{2}$ is the number of pairs of such individuals. Summing over all elements of the matrix (except those in the diagonal), we have

$$\sum_{\substack{i,j=1 \\ (j \neq i)}}^{n} \binom{b_{ij}}{2}$$

as the total number of agreements between pairs of individuals. A measure of consensus can now be defined as

$$u = \frac{2\sum_{\substack{i,j=1 \\ (j \neq i)}}^{n} \binom{b_{ij}}{2}}{\binom{N}{2}\binom{n}{2}} - 1$$

$$= \frac{8\sum \binom{b_{ij}}{2}}{N(N-1)\,n(n-1)} - 1$$

This measure is known as the "coefficient of agreement." If and only if there is complete agreement, $u = 1$. Minimum consensus arises when half the individuals prefer A_i to A_j and the other half prefer A_j to A_i, for all values of i and j. In this case all the elements of the matrix are $N/2$ if N is even, or $(N \pm 1)/2$ if N is odd. If these values are substituted for b_{ij} in the formula for u, we find that

$$\min u = \frac{-1}{N-1} \quad \text{if N is even}$$

$$= \frac{-1}{N} \quad \text{if N is odd}$$

Thus the smallest possible value of u is -1 and can arise only when $N = 2$. As N increases, min u approaches zero.

Consensus and the theory of collective decisions

Finally, we mention a special kind of consensus among preference rankings which is important in the theory of collective decisions.

This theory deals with the problem of aggregating individual preferences to produce social preferences. The central problem, first stated in a general form by Kenneth Arrow in his now famous Impossibility Theorem, concerns the existence of a "social welfare function" or "group decision rule"; that is, a mapping which, subject to certain conditions, associates with each set of individual preference rankings a social ranking of the alternatives (Arrow 1963). Briefly, Arrow has shown that a decision rule which satisfies certain very reasonable conditions and yields a transitive social ordering of the alternatives does not in general exist.[10]

It has been found, however, that if a special kind of consensus exists among the individuals (which implies a restriction on one of Arrow's conditions), there then exists at least one decision rule — simple majority rule — which satisfies Arrow's other conditions. This fundamental result is due to Duncan Black, whose theorem, generalized by Arrow, is essentially as follows. If the individual preference rankings satisfy the single-peakedness condition, then majority decision is an acceptable decision rule— that is, it does not lead to intransitive social preferences.[11] The set of individual rankings is said to satisfy the single-peakedness condition if there is an underlying ordering of the alternative such that, in passing from left to right in this underlying order, each individual rises monotonically to the peak of his preferences and then drops monotonically.[12]

10. For an introduction to the problem and a survey of the literature, see Luce and Raiffa 1957, chapter 14; and Riker 1961, pp. 900-11.

11. See Black 1958; Arrow 1963, chapter 7; and Luce and Raiffa 1957, section 14.7.

12. In Coombsian terms, this is equivalent to the existence of an "underlying qualitative joint scale." See Coombs 1964, chapter 18.

Single-peakedness is a special kind of consensus. It results from the alternatives being viewed in the same way by all the individuals — in the sense that, in ranking the alternatives, they appear to use the same criterion. This criterion corresponds to the underlying one-dimensional ordering (or scale) which generates the individual preferences.[13]

It can easily be shown that the existence of this type of consensus is quite independent of the consensus defined above by the coefficient of concordance. To take an extreme example, if half the individuals rank four alternatives as (A_1, A_2, A_3, A_4), and the other half rank them in exactly the reverse order, i.e., (A_4, A_3, A_2, A_1), then we find that $W = 0$ (the minimum value for concordance). However, the rankings are single-peaked, the underlying order being (A_1, A_2, A_3, A_4) or its reverse.[14]

13. Other conditions, which are restrictions on the admissible individual rankings and imply some kind of similarity among the rankings, have been discovered recently. The most general is Sen's condition of "value-restricted preferences." See Sen 1966, pp. 491–99.

14. Anthony Downs (1957, p. 62) writes of the "extreme degree of consensus among voters on every detail of every issue" which would be necessary if the Arrow problem is not to arise. Such extreme consensus is not necessary, since, as we have seen, the single-peakedness condition may be satisfied even when there is very little consensus (in the usual sense).

BIBLIOGRAPHY

Alford, Robert R. 1967. Class voting in the Anglo-American political systems. In Party systems and voter alignments, ed. S. M. Lipset and Stein Rokkan, chapter 1. New York: Free Press.

————. 1963. Party and society. Chicago: Rand McNally.

Allardt, Erik, and Littunen, Yrjo, eds. 1964. Cleavages, ideologies, and party systems. Helsinki: Academic Bookstore.

Allardt, Erik, and Pesonen, P. 1967. Cleavages in Finnish politics. In Party systems and voter alignments, ed. S. M. Lipset and Stein Rokkan, chapter 7. New York: Free Press.

Almond, Gabriel. 1960. The politics of the developing areas, introduction. Princeton, N.J.: Princeton University Press.

Almond, Gabriel, and Verba, Sidney. 1965. The civic culture. Boston: Little, Brown.

Anderson, Lee F., Watts, Merideth W., and Wilcox, Allen R. 1965. Legislative roll call analysis. Evanston, Ill.: Northwestern University Press.

Armstrong, W. E. 1951. Utility and the theory of welfare. Oxford Economic Papers N.S. 3.

Arrow, Kenneth J. 1963. Social choice and individual values. 2nd ed. New York: Wiley.

Axelrod, Robert. 1968. Conflict of interest: theory and political applications. Ph.D. diss. Yale University.

Barker, Ernest. 1958. Reflections on government. New York: Oxford University Press.

Bentley, Arthur F. 1908. The process of government. Chicago: University of Chicago Press.

Black, Duncan. 1958. The theory of committees and elections. Cambridge: Cambridge University Press.

Blalock, Hubert M. 1960. Social statistics. New York: McGraw-Hill.

Brams, Steven, and O'Leary, Michael. 1968.   A mathe-
    matical model of voting bodies.   Mimeograph.   Syra-
    cuse University, Department of Political Science.
Budge, Ian. 1970.   Democratic agreement and democratic
    stability.   Chicago: Markham.
Campbell, Angus, and Valen, Henry. 1966.   Party identi-
    fication in Norway and the United States. In Campbell,
    Angus, Converse, Philip E., Miller, Warren E., and
    Stokes, Donald E., Elections and the political order,
    chapter 13.   New York: Wiley.
Campbell, Angus, Gurin, Gerald, and Miller, Warren E.
    1954.   The voter decides.   Evanston, Ill.: Row, Peter-
    son.
Cantril, Hadley. 1946.   The intensity of an attitude.   J.
    abnorm. soc. Psychol. 41.
Converse, Philip E. 1966. The problem of party distances
    in models of voting change.   In The electoral process,
    ed. M. Kent Jennings and L. Harmon Zeigler, chapter
    9.   Englewood Cliffs, N.J.: Prentice-Hall.
Coombs, Clyde H. 1964. Theory of data, chapter 18. New
    York: Wiley.
Coser, Lewis A. 1956.   The functions of social conflict.
    Glencoe, Ill.: Free Press.
Dahl, Robert. 1956. A preface to democratic theory. Chi-
    cago: University of Chicago Press.
————. 1961. Who governs? Democracy and power in an
    American city.   New Haven: Yale University Press.
Dahl, Robert, and Lindblom, Edward.   1953.   Politics,
    economics and welfare.   New York: Harper & Row.
Dahrendorf, Ralf. 1959.   Class and class conflict in in-
    dustrial society. Stanford, Calif.: Stanford University
    Press.
Derge, David R. 1959.   Urban-rural conflict: the case of
    Illinois.   In Legislative behavior, ed. John Walke and
    Heinz Eulau, pp. 218–27.   Glencoe, Ill.: Free Press.
Downs, Anthony. 1957.   Economic theory of democracy.
    New York: Harper & Row.
Galtung, Johan. 1967.   Theory and methods of social re-
    search.   Oslo: Universitetsforlaget.

Goodman, Leo, and Kruskal, William H. 1954. Measures of association for cross classifications. J. Amer. statist. Ass. 49.

—————. 1959. Measures of association for cross classifications II. J. Amer. statist. Ass. 54.

Goodman, L. A., and Markowitz, H. 1952. Social welfare functions based on individual rankings. Amer. J. Sociology 57.

Greenberg, Joseph H. 1956. The measurement of linguistic diversity. Language 32.

Griffith, E. S., Plamenatz, J., and Pennock, J. R. 1956. Cultural prerequisites to a successfully functioning democracy. Amer. Pol. Sci. Rev. 50.

Hall, N., and Tideman, N. 1967. Measures of Concentration. J. Amer. statist. Ass. 62.

Hempel, Carl G. 1952. Fundamentals of concept formation in empirical science. Chicago: University of Chicago Press.

Jacobson, Kurt. 1967. Voting behavior of the Nordic countries in the General Assembly. Cooperation and Conflict 3–4.

Kalela, Jaakko. 1967. The Nordic group in the General Assembly. Cooperation and Conflict 3–4.

Kaplan, Abraham. 1964. The conduct of inquiry. San Francisco: Chandler.

Katz, Daniel. 1944. The measurement of intensity. In Gauging public opinion, ed. Hadley Cantril, chapter 3.

Kendall, Maurice G. 1962. Rank correlation methods. 3rd ed. London: Griffin.

Kendall, Willmoore, and Carey, George W. 1968. The intensity problem and democratic theory. Amer. Pol. Sci. Rev. 62.

Kesselman, Mark. 1966. French local politics: a statistical examination of grassroots consensus. Amer. Pol. Sci. Rev. 60.

Key, V. O. 1964. Public opinion and American democracy, chapter 9. New York: Knopf.

—————. 1949. Southern politics. New York: Knopf.

Kornhauser, Robert. 1959. Politics of mass society. Glencoe, Ill.: Free Press.

150

Lane, Robert E. 1959. Political life. New York: Free Press.

Lane, Robert E., and Sears, David. 1964. Public opinion. Englewood Cliffs, N.J.: Prentice-Hall.

Lasswell, Harold. 1936. Politics: who gets what, when, how? New York: McGraw-Hill.

Lazarsfeld, P. F., Berelson, B., and Graudet, Hazel. 1944. The people's choice. New York: Columbia University Press.

Leik, Robert K. 1966. A measure of ordinal consensus. Pacific Sociological Rev. 9.

Levy, Marion. 1952. The structure of society. Princeton, N.J.: Princeton University Press.

Lidstrom, Jan-Erik, and Wiklund, Claes. 1967. The Nordic countries in the General Assembly and its two political committees. Cooperation and Conflict 3-4.

Lijphart, Arend. 1963. The analysis of bloc voting in the General Assembly: a critique and a proposal. Amer. Pol. Sci. Rev. 58.

————. 1968. The politics of accommodation. Berkeley and Los Angeles: University of California Press.

Lipset, Seymour Martin. 1960. Political man. Garden City, N.Y.: Doubleday.

Lipset, Seymour Martin, and Rokkan, Stein, eds. 1967. Party systems and voter alignments. New York: Free Press.

Luce, R. Duncan, and Raiffa, Howard. 1957. Games and decisions. New York: Wiley.

McCloskey, Herbert. 1964. Consensus and ideology in American politics. Amer. Pol. Sci. Rev. 58.

Mitchell, William C. 1963. Interest group theory and 'overlapping memberships': a critique. Paper read at the annual meeting of the American Political Science Association.

Prothro, James W., and Grigg, Charles M. 1960. Fundamental principles of democracy: bases of agreement and disagreement. J. Politics 22.

Rae, Douglas, and Taylor, Michael. 1969. Some ambiguities in the concept of 'intensity.' Polity 1.

Rice, Stuart. 1925. The behavior of legislative groups. Pol. Sci. Quart. 40.

————. 1949. Quantitative methods in politics. New York: Knopf.

Rieselbach, Leroy. 1960. Quantitative methods for studying voting behavior in the General Assembly. Int. Org.

Riker, William H. 1965. Arrow's theorem and some examples of the paradox of voting. In Mathematical applications in political science, ed. John M. Claunch. Dallas: Southern Methodist University, Arnold Foundation.

————. 1961. Voting and the summation of preferences. Amer. Pol. Sci. Rev. 55.

Ross, Edward. 1920. The principles of sociology. New York: Century.

Rothenberg, Jerome. 1961. The measurement of social welfare, part III. Englewood Cliffs, N.J.: Prentice-Hall.

Russett, Bruce, et al. 1964. World handbook of political and social indicators. New Haven: Yale University Press.

Sen, Amartya K. 1966. A possibility theorem on majority decisions. Econometrica 34.

Shannon, Claude E., and Weaver, Warren. 1964. The mathematical theory of communication. Urbana: University of Illinois Press.

Siegel, Sidney. 1956. Nonparametric statistics for the behavioral sciences. New York: McGraw-Hill.

Simmel, Georg. 1955. Conflict and the web of group affiliations, trans. Kurt H. Wolff. Glencoe, Ill.: Free Press.

Simon, Herbert A. 1954. Spurious correlations: a causal interpretation. J. Amer. statist. Ass. 49.

Simpson, E. H. 1949. Measurement of diversity. Nature 163.

Somit, Albert, and Tannenhaus, Joseph. 1967. The development of American political science. Boston: Allyn and Bacon.

Stokes, Donald E. 1963. Spatial models of party competition. Amer. Pol. Sci. Rev. 57.

Stouffer, S. A., et al. 1950.   Measurement and prediction
(Studies in social psychology in World War II, vol.4).
Princeton, N.J.: Princeton University Press.

Tingsten, Herbert. 1937.   Political behavior: studies in
election statistics.   London: King.

Truman, David B. 1951. The governmental process. New
York: Knopf.

United Nations' statistical yearbook. Year as cited. New
York.

Winch, Peter. 1958.   The idea of a social science, p. 89.
London: Routledge and Kegan Paul.

Yearbook of labor statistics 1965. 1966.   Geneva: International Labor Office.